GREAT BEERS
AND PUBS ALONG
THE ROUTE TO
CANTERBURY

ROGER PROTZ

THE
CANTERBURY
ALES

GREAT BEERS
AND PUBS ALONG
THE ROUTE TO
CANTERBURY

First published 2022

The History Press
97 St George's Place, Cheltenham,
Gloucestershire, GL50 3QB
www.thehistorypress.co.uk

British Library Cataloguing in Publication Data.
A catalogue record for this book is available from the British Library.

ISBN 978 0 7509 9214 5

Typesetting and origination by The History Press
Printed and bound in Great Britain by TJ Books Limited, Padstow, Cornwall.

MIX
Paper from
responsible sources
FSC   FSC® C013056
www.fsc.org

Trees for LYfe

Contents

Introduction

Now as I've drunk a draught of corn-ripe ale,
By God it stands to reason I can strike
On some good story that you all will like.

Geoffrey Chaucer, *The Canterbury Tales*

This book was inspired by Chaucer's fourteenth-century master-piece that, through the stories recounted by his pilgrims, paints a vivid portrait of medieval England. Tales that are bawdy, ribald, courtly and elegant show what life was like at all levels of society.

As the pilgrims gathered in an inn in London and ate, drank and slept in inns on their journey to Canterbury, I thought it would be fascinating to follow in their footsteps and visit the modern pubs and breweries along the way.

My personal pilgrimage is timely, as the world of brewing has changed dramatically in the twenty-first century. Changes in the way beer is taxed – known as excise duty – means small brewers pay less than bigger ones and this has led to the growth of a dynamic craft sector, offering consumers a far better choice and variety of beers. While Shepherd Neame in Faversham is a traditional family brewer, there are now many new and smaller producers in the region. The list of brewers in south London alone at the end of the first chapter is an indication of the size and scope of the new sector.

The guide was compiled in exceptional circumstances. I had made good progress when the covid-19 pandemic struck. It meant travel was restricted and pubs were closed during lockdown. I resumed my work in the summer and early autumn of 2021.

The pubs in the book fall into two categories: tied houses and free houses. A tied house means it is owned by either a brewer or a non-brewing pub company and both will decide the beers publicans can sell. Free houses are independent and publicans can choose their own beers. Some brewers and pub companies allow publicans to offer customers guest beers and such beers can change on a regular basis.

This book is not a comprehensive pub guide. I have chosen a selection of pubs that offer good beer and, in many cases, good food as well as interesting stories that reflect the history of their areas. Readers planning visits and who would like a bigger choice of pubs should use the CAMRA online facility whatpub?

There is a second trail to Canterbury called the Pilgrims' Way. This begins in Winchester and makes its way to Canterbury through Hampshire, Surrey and parts of Kent, avoiding London. I have followed this route, too, and found a wealth of fine pubs and many new breweries, including Hogs Back that has developed its own hop fields and revived a once-famous hop variety, the Farnham White Bine.

I have also included a section on Maidstone, the county town of Kent, which once had major breweries and where the Goacher family has restored pride to the town.

Roger Protz, St Albans, 2022

Part 1:
The London to
Kent Route
of the Pilgrims

In the Beginning:
Southwark and the
Old Kent Road

But first I make a protestation round
That I'm quite drunk. I know it by my sound
And therefore, if I slander or mis-say
Blame it on ale of Southwark so I pray.

The Miller's Tale

George Inn, off 77 Borough High Street, London SE1. The George is a glorious emblem of medieval and Elizabethan London and it stands almost precisely where Chaucer's book begins, for it was just a few yards from another great inn, the Tabard, where the pilgrims gathered in 1385. The antiquarian John Stow, in his Survey of London in 1598, records that Southwark was once crowded with inns, including the Spire, the Christopher, the Bull, the Queen's Head, the Tabard, the George, the Hart and the King's Head.

And all the inns were close to Southwark Cathedral, where Thomas Becket gave his last sermon before heading to Canterbury and his death.

The Tabard was next door to the George on the east side of Borough High Street. In common with all the inns in and around the Borough, it was a large and roistering place, packed with strolling musicians, drunks, thieves and prostitutes as well as the more serious-minded who were setting off to pay homage to Thomas Becket in Canterbury. Picture Mistress Quickly's Boar's Head in Shakespeare's *Henry IV* and other plays, where Falstaff and his cronies boozed and whored, and you may have an image not too far removed from that of the real-life Tabard.

In medieval times, Southwark was beyond the jurisdiction of the City of London. In the city, such activities as prostitution and animal baiting were banned but they were unconstrained in Southwark. As a result, the area became the capital's entertainment centre and people hurried there to indulge in all the pleasures of the flesh.

The Tabard was built in 1307 as a London residence for the Abbot of Hyde in Kent. The Tabard and its neighbouring inns were close to the junction of two Roman roads, Stane Street and Watling Street, and the entire area was part of the Manor of Southwark controlled by the bishops of Winchester: prostitutes who worked in the area were known as 'Winchester Geese', a soubriquet that was probably kept well hidden from the bishops.

This image of the Tabard, renamed the Talbot, dates from around 1850, shortly before it was demolished. The name Ind Coope refers to the then owners, a brewery based in Romford, Essex. (historic-uk.com)

When the pilgrims met there in 1385, the inn was owned by a man with the remarkably modern-sounding name of Harry Bailly, who clearly ran a popular place to meet, eat, drink and sleep. Chaucer wrote:

> It happened in that season that one day
> In Southwark, at the Tabard, as I lay
> Ready to go on pilgrimage and start
> For Canterbury, most devout at heart,
> At night there came into that hostelry
> Some nine and twenty in a company
> Of sundry folk happening to fall
> In fellowship, and they were pilgrims all
> That towards Canterbury meant to ride.
> The rooms and stables of the inn were wide;
> They made us easy, all was of the best.

In 1676, ten years after the Great Fire of London, another contagion known as the Great Fire of Southwark destroyed or badly damaged many of the local inns, including the Tabard and the George. The Tabard was rebuilt but was renamed the Talbot. In common with other inns in Southwark, the Talbot did good business at the height of coach travel in the eighteenth and early nineteenth centuries but it went into rapid decline with the arrival of the railway and London Bridge station next door and eventually closed.

The George, first called the George and Dragon in honour of England's patron saint, is the only great galleried London coaching inn to have survived both the great fire and the coming of the railway. It was rebuilt in 1677 and once occupied three sides of the courtyard off the high street. But in the great railway boom of the nineteenth century, Guy's Hospital, by then the owner of the inn, sold it to the London and North Eastern Railway Company and

The George.

the railway barons, in an act of appalling vandalism, tore down part of the site to make way for engine sheds. Fortunately there is still a spacious inn to admire and it is looked after with greater care and reverence by its current owner, the National Trust. The trust has won for it the status of Grade I listed to stop any further acts of cultural terrorism.

The ground floor bars of the George are small and low-ceilinged with latticed windows, beams, bare boards and wooden settles. The Parliament Bar, nearest the street, was once the waiting room for coach passengers. It has a Parliamentary Clock, a reminder of the time in 1797 when parliament, in one of its periodic mad moods, imposed taxes on timepieces. The middle bar was known as the Coffee Room in the nineteenth century and was used regularly by Charles Dickens, who mentioned the George in *Little Dorrit*. Southwark and the Borough also featured in *A Tale of Two Cities*, with coaches setting off along the Old Dover Road.

A narrow corridor leads to a more spacious bar at the rear of the inn, where visitors can dine as well as drink. Narrow stairs lead up to more dining rooms with views of the courtyard from the first-floor galleries. In fine weather, excerpts from Shakespeare's plays are performed from both the galleries and the courtyard. Morris Men also perform their arcane rituals in the yard, where benches and seats are set out for eating and drinking.

Blue Plaque in Talbot Yard.

The George is run for the National Trust by the Suffolk brewer Greene King. The brewery dates from 1799 and as it's based in Bury St Edmunds it adds its own long and fascinating history to the inn. You can enjoy its range of beers that includes IPA and Abbot Ale along with seasonal brews and guest beers from other breweries, including the sublime Landlord from Timothy Taylor in Yorkshire.

It's easy to miss the George. As you walk south from London Bridge along Borough High Street, watch out for the inn sign at the entrance to a narrow passage that leads to the courtyard. There's a further piece of history across the road from the George. The Hop Exchange at 24 Southwark Street was built in 1867 to allow brewers and hop merchants to meet and discuss the price of hops brought from the Kent countryside. The Grade II-listed building was bombed during the Second World War and the remaining floors are now used as offices but, with its vast main floor and hop motifs and artefacts, it serves to underscore the importance of brewing in Southwark.

The name the Tabard is not forgotten. A few minutes further south from the George brings you to Tabard Street, where you will find the **Royal Oak** (44 Tabard Street, SE1: transport Borough Underground). This splendid pub is a no-nonsense, unspoilt, traditional London boozer with two bars, a serving hatch and the full range of beers from the owner, Harvey's brewery in Lewes, East Sussex. Alongside the acclaimed Sussex Best Bitter you will find Mild and IPA plus regular guest beers. Imaginative food is cooked with ingredients brought from Borough Market. It's the ideal place to raise a glass to the memory of the Tabard inn.

The area is rich in history. Tabard Street meets Pilgrimage Street and both merge into the roar of Great Dover Street that soon becomes the Old Kent Road: we are on the A2 and definitively on our way to Canterbury. Chaucer records that the pilgrims paused to refresh themselves and their horses at a 'watering hole' on the road. Watering hole today is common parlance for a pub but for the pilgrims and their mounts it was a source of water called the Earl's Sluice, a tributary of the River Peck that gives its name to Peckham.

It's likely that, over the following centuries, inns may have been built on the spot but the current imposing three-storey building, topped by a Dutch gable, the **Thomas à Becket,** 320–322 Old Kent Road, SE5, dates from 1898. The pub achieved fame in the late twentieth century as it had a large gym where professional boxers trained: there's a blue plaque to mark the achievements of Sir Henry Cooper, who fought and almost defeated Muhammad Ali – then known as Cassius Clay – in 1963. Music rehearsals were also held there and David Bowie was among the singers who used the facilities.

Royal Oak, Tabard Street.

Nor forgotten: the former Thomas a Becket pub, Old Kent Road, still has Becket on the sign.

The pub ran into hard times, closed and for a while was an estate agent's. It was in danger of being demolished but it was rescued by the Walworth Society, which gained an Asset of Community Value from the local council. An ACV is a type of listing and it meant the building couldn't be fundamentally altered. It reopened as a bar and grill that failed and it's now a Vietnamese restaurant called Viet Quan. Fortunately the pub sign remains and it's a reproduction of the image of Becket in a stained glass window in Canterbury Cathedral.

The pub claims to be one of the most haunted buildings in London and even usually brave souls refuse to visit the upper floors at night. The ghosts are said to include three nuns from the Sisters of Mercy who wander the second floor whispering to themselves.

Before heading for the sylvan pleasures of Greenwich and Blackheath, the pilgrims' next stop was Deptford. In their time it was a small fishing village on the Thames but it became an important dockyard from the sixteenth century. Henry VIII was responsible for the first Royal Dockyard there and its importance can be measured by the fact that Elizabeth I knighted Francis Drake on board the *Golden Hind* in 1581.

The area had a seamy side and the playwright Christopher Marlowe was murdered there in 1593. He's buried in St Nicholas church and there's a plaque on his grave.

Dog and Bell,
Deptford.

Eventually the royal dockyards moved to Greenwich and Deptford declined as an industrial area: an anchor in the high street marks its historic connections. There's one excellent pub, the **Dog & Bell,** 116 Prince Street, SE8, formerly the Royal Marine. It has a good reputation for food and drink and stages an annual pickle festival. The pub is listed in the CAMRA Good Beer Guide and has Fuller's London Pride as a regular beer along with several guest ales.

BERMONDSEY BREWERIES

In Chaucer's time, the Old Kent Road and surrounding areas were rich in inns and breweries. The brewing tradition has been revived in the twenty-first century with a number of small craft breweries setting up shop in the area. There's an Old Kent Road Brewery that has led a peripatetic existence and at the time of writing is based on a different but equally historic thoroughfare, Jamaica Road. The name marked the important trade the London docks conducted with the Caribbean.

An informal Bermondsey Beer Walk has sprung up, with beer lovers spending Saturday afternoons visiting some of the breweries and beer shops in the area and sampling the brews. They include:

Southwark Brewery, 46 Druid Street, SE1
Barrel Project, 80 Druid Street, SE1
Anspach & Hobday, 118 Druid Street, SE1
Brew by Numbers, 79 Enid Street, SE16
Cloudwater, 73 Enid Street, SE16
Moor Beer, 71 Enid Street, SE16
The Kernel, Arch 11, Dockley Road Industrial Estate, Dockley Road, SE16
Partizan, 34 Raymouth Road, SE16
Fourpure, 22 Bermondsey Trading Estate, Rotherhithe New Road, SE16
Hiver, 56 Stanworth Street, SE1
Spartan, 8 Almond Road, SE16

Deptford has Brick Brewery, Units 13–14, Deptford Trading Estate, Blackhorse Road, SE8. It also has a taproom in the arches of the former Peckham railway station.

The Old Kent Road is poorly served by train and Underground but there are plenty of buses that take you back to London Bridge and central London. Deptford has a train station, while Deptford Bridge is on the Docklands Light Railway. The Old Kent Road station closed during the First World War. A station called New Bermondsey is planned, while an extension to the Bakerloo Line may stop at either Old Kent Road or Peckham Rye.

Greenwich and Blackheath

Chaucer records that following a pause for water on the Old Kent Road and a short stay in Deptford, the pilgrims headed towards Greenwich. Historically we are now entering Kent: Greenwich and neighbouring Blackheath were part of the county of Kent until they were absorbed into London during local government reorganisation in the twentieth century. In Greenwich the pilgrims were alongside the mighty waterway of the River Thames and there was no shortage of inns and taverns where they were able to rest and dine in the robust company of sailors and men working on ships and river boats. The hostelries were no doubt known to the Friar among the Pilgrims: Chaucer says: 'He knew the taverns well in every town/And every innkeeper and barmaid too.'

Today the area known as Maritime Greenwich is a UNESCO World Heritage Site and is dominated by the magnificent Old Royal Naval College designed by Sir Christopher Wren. Before the college was built it had been the site of a royal palace since the fifteenth century. Several Tudor monarchs were born there, including Henry VIII and Elizabeth I, and in later life they visited the palace regularly, coming by boat from Westminster.

The palace was demolished during the English Civil War and was replaced by the Royal Naval Hospital for sick sailors, designed by Wren. The extended buildings became the Old Royal Naval College in 1873 and they are now home to the University of Greenwich and a music school. The complex includes the **Old**

Old Brewery, Greenwich.

Brewery, Pepys Building, SE10, which has a long and fascinating history. The royal palace included a brewery that produced ale for Henry VIII and other monarchs. When the naval college replaced the palace, a new brewery was installed in 1717 to supply beer for elderly and sick sailors: beer was piped to the cellars of the Pensioners' Room in the Queen Mary Building. The seamen were allowed three pints a day and it's thought the beer was porter; a strong, dark and nutritious ale, of which the strongest version was called stout porter, later reduced to just stout.

In 1833 Joseph Kay and John Braithwaite built a new brew house with a steam engine that ground grain and pumped water: before that time, motive power was provided by horses. Ten years later the brewery was badly damaged by fire and was rebuilt and reinforced with brick arches and iron girders that are still in place today. The brewery closed around 1870 but brewing was

Brewing kit at Old Brewery, Greenwich.

restored in 2010 by the Meantime Brewery in Greenwich.

Master brewer Alastair Hook installed new vessels used to recreate old beer styles, including porter, with some beers aged in wooden casks. Brewing ceased yet again when Meantime was bought by the Japanese brewer Asahi and the Old Brewery was sold to the London pub company Young's of Wandsworth. The bar serves Young's Original and Special, brewed by Marston's, along with a guest beer such as St Austell Proper Job.

The brew house is now a spacious restaurant with top-quality food. The brewing vessels are still in place and Young's is considering restarting brewing. Food and drink can also be enjoyed in a large beer garden, while next door to the restaurant Discover Greenwich traces the history of the area. The building housing both the brewery and Discover Greenwich is called the Pepys Building to commemorate Samuel Pepys: as well as being a famous diarist he was also the Administrator of the Navy for the government in the seventeenth century.

The work of John Kay can also been seen at the Grade II-listed **Trafalgar Tavern,** Park Row, SE10, just a few minutes' walk from the Pepys Building. Kay designed this opulent three-storey build-ing alongside the Thames in the 1830s with balconies and galleries along with impressive chandeliers in the stately rooms. The tavern was known to Charles Dickens, who set the wedding breakfast scene there in *Our Mutual Friend*. The Liberal Party held an annual whitebait dinner at the tavern in the nine-teenth century. It became a home for old sailors in the First World War and was a working men's club between the two world wars. It

Trafalgar Tavern.

must surely have been the most luxurious club in the country.

The Trafalgar reopened as a pub and restaurant in 1965 and in 1996 it was voted Best London Pub by the *London Evening Standard*. Today, with its bars, restaurants and ballroom, it's a popular venue for weddings and conferences. It's fronted at the river end by a statue of Lord Nelson and inside the bar has two house beers in his honour, Nelson IPA and Trafalgar Bitter, along with three beers from the Suffolk brewer Adnams: Ghost Ship, Lighthouse and Southwold Bitter.

Both the Old Brewery and the Trafalgar Tavern are close to the birth of the world-famous nineteenth century tea clipper, *Cutty Sark*. The ship has been badly damaged by fire twice in the twenty-first century but it has been restored and is open to visitors. It has its own stop on the Docklands Light Railway.

The **Plume of Feathers,** 19 Park Vista, SE10, is the oldest inn in Greenwich and dates from 1691. It stood originally on the Old Dover Road, where it acted as a coaching inn, but the route was redirected by a local aristocrat. Today the pub is just a few minutes' walk from Maze Hill station and is a few yards from the National Maritime Museum. There are seats on the pavement, where customers are welcomed by hanging baskets filled with lavish floral

Plume of Feathers.

displays. Inside the pub is decorated with old maritime artefacts and photos of the local area. There's a large beer garden and the food in a separate restaurant is recommended. Beers include Adnams Southwold Bitter and Harvey's Sussex Best.

There is much for visitors to see in Greenwich and local walking tours are available. Greenwich Village has many fine Regency buildings and restaurants, while the Meridian Line marks Greenwich Mean Time, from which the world measures different time zones. The area also houses the Royal Observatory and the O2 Millennium Dome, home to regular music and sporting events. The area is well served by public transport, with Greenwich, Cutty Sark and Maze Hill stations.

But now, in common with the Pilgrims, we must move on to Blackheath, best reached today by the 386 bus. Whether you make the short journey from Greenwich by bus or horse, you are bedazzled as you approach by the great sweep of the heath land that drops down into a dale dotted with church steeples and streets of fine Georgian and Victorian houses. This is one of the most sort-after areas of London where locals can enjoy one of the biggest areas of common land in Greater London.

It's a fine area for recreation and no doubt the Pilgrims wined and dined well on their visit. With so much wide open space, Blackheath has long been a centre for sport. The first golf club in England was founded here in 1766 and it was an important centre for cricket for many years. Large crowds watched keenly fought games between Kent and London and Kent versus All-England. The first game between Kent and London was played in 1730 at a time when wickets had just two stumps, bowling was under-arm and bats were curved like hockey sticks.

These sylvan delights had their darker side. In 1381, just a few years before the Pilgrims set off for Canterbury, large parts of England were in the grip of a major rebellion, the Peasants' Revolt led by a man of Kent, Wat Tyler. Seventy years later, Jack Cade's

Rebellion in 1450 attempted to take London and overthrow the monarchy. In both cases, Blackheath was a rallying point for the large bodies of men involved in the rebellions (see following section). The heath is crossed by the old Roman road, Watling Street, which took coaches down to Kent and the Channel ports. In the seventeenth and eighteenth centuries, the heath was a notorious haunt of highwaymen, who stopped coaches at gun point and robbed their passengers. If caught, the robbers were given short shrift and the heath was once dotted with gibbets where felons were hanged and left to rot.

On a happier note, the Pilgrims would have approved of our first pub, **Zero Degrees**, 29 Montpelier Vale, SE3. It's a modern bar but it brews its own beer, which was a common practice in the fourteenth century. The Blackheath pub is the first of a small chain of four specialist home-brew bars where the brewing equipment is on view to customers, in this case to the rear of the ground floor. Seating at the front has fine views to the left of the heath, with handsome houses across the road.

Food is good, imaginative, plentiful and well-priced: there are often meal-and-drink deals. The brewery produces three regular

Zero Degrees.

beers – Bohemian Czech Pilsner, Downtown American IPA and Our Mango Beer – with a new additional beer every month. The beers are unfiltered and are suitable for vegetarians.

Zero Degrees brewing kit.

From Zero Degrees, turn right down the steep drop into Blackheath Village. At a junction turn left and you will find the **Railway** at 16 Blackheath Village, SE3, a few yards from the train station. The large pub is a good example of the inns that sprang up in the nineteenth century as the iron way transformed travel in Britain and quickly put horse-drawn coaches and coaching inns out of business.

The Blackheath pub is part of the Ember Inns chain. It has a spacious interior, with wooden floors, comfortable seating, pastel-painted walls and a partitioned drinking area at the front where drinkers can nuzzle a pint and read a newspaper. There's plenti-

The Railway.

ful food, a courtyard at the rear and many old photos of the area. Regular beers include Fuller's London Pride and Sharp's Doom Bar, while guest ales may be St Austell Proper Job or Taylor's Landlord. The station has trains back to London Bridge and Cannon Street.

Rebels with a Cause

Blackheath has strong associations with Wat Tyler and the Peasants' Revolt of 1381 and Jack Cade's Rebellion of 1450. The first revolt was sparked by a poll tax that levied four pence on all men regardless of income and status. It brought to a head long-simmering discontent by peasants, who wanted greater freedom to work for employers of their choice rather than being tied to just one landowner. The peasants were inspired by the preaching of a radical priest, John Ball, who said all men and women were descended from Adam and Eve and were therefore equal before God. He coined the famous lines: 'When Adam delved and Eve span/Who was then the gentleman?'

Walter or Wat Tyler is said to have come either from Essex or Kent but it's thought his family were based in Dartford or Maidstone. He emerged as the leader of the revolt and took a group of peasants from Canterbury to Blackheath, where they were joined by more supporters. They marched on London, where looting broke out, prisons were opened and Savoy Palace, home of the deeply unpopular John of Gaunt, Duke of Lancaster, was sacked.

Richard II, then 14 years of age, met the rebels and agreed to meet some of their demands. Tyler was not satisfied and a second meeting was held at Smithfield. Tyler spoke directly to the king but was accused of insulting the monarch as a result of his rude manner. A fight broke out and Tyler was badly wounded. He was taken to hospital but supporters of the king removed him and decapitated him. His head was paraded around London on a pole and then displayed on London Bridge. King Richard revoked all the concessions he had made to the peasants.

There are several memorials to Tyler. There's a Wat Tyler Road in Blackheath and a section of the A249 through Maidstone is called Wat Tyler Way. Wat Tyler's Causeway in Hertfordshire runs from Newgate Street towards the A1000, marking the route taken by the peasants after laying siege to St Albans Abbey. There's a Wat Tyler Country Park in Essex and a memorial stone with his name in Smithfield Market.

Jack Cade, known as the Captain of Kent, led an army of 5,000 people who assembled on Blackheath before marching in London. They were complaining about corruption and abuse of power by Henry VI's advisors. Against Cade's wishes, looting broke out and the citizens of the capital rose up and drove the rebels back to London Bridge. Cade made his escape from London but was caught by the High Sheriff of Kent. In the ensuing struggle, Cade was badly wounded and died before he could be taken to London to stand trial. His followers were ruthlessly hounded and caught in Blackheath, Canterbury, Faversham and Maidstone.

Dartford

Dartford has long been an important resting place for pilgrims heading to Canterbury. Watling Street, the old Roman road, goes through the town that today remains a major transport hub, with the Dartford Crossing on the M25 linking Kent with Thurrock in Essex on the other bank of the Thames 20 miles away.

Chaucer's pilgrims would have found no shortage of inns for accommodation in the town. They would also have had a good choice of ales to drink, for Dartford has a long history of brewing. This is shown by the local council's decision, when it was redesigning the town centre, to rename Market Street Brewery Square.

Commercial breweries operated from the seventeenth century. The last major brewery started life as Miller & Aldworth and was renamed the Dartford Brewery in 1897. It was bought by a succession of bigger breweries in Kent and London and closed in 1970. But brewing has been restored to the area with the Dartford Wobblers Brewery (see below).

Both princes and paupers have enriched Dartford's history. During the Peasants' Revolt, large groups of Wat Tyler's rebels from both Essex and Kent gathered in the town in 1381 and then made their way to Rochester and Canterbury to link up with other supporters. In 1415, Henry V marched in triumph with his troops through Dartford en route to London after his famous victory in France at Agincourt.

His son, Henry VI, was also involved in the town. During his tumultuous reign, bedevilled by the Wars of the Roses between the houses of Lancaster and York, one of his rivals, Richard, Duke of York, assembled an army of 10,000 men in Dartford in preparation for an attempt to seize the throne. In spite of having such a large force, Richard surrendered to the king in the town: York Road marks the spot.

Dartford's early economy was based on agriculture but it became a busy industrial town in the nineteenth and twentieth centuries with flour and paper mills, chemical works and a Vickers aircraft plant. Those industries have disappeared in our post-industrial society and today it's best known for the great sprawl of the Bluewater shopping centre just outside the town. It occupies 240 acres and is one of the biggest shopping malls in the world. It provides jobs for many local people. Others commute swiftly into London by train.

Dartford has strong connections to rock 'n' roll. Both Mick Jagger and Keith Richards of the Rolling Stones were born in the town, as was Sir Peter Blake, the artist and graphic designer best known for his cover for the Beatles' *Sgt Pepper* album.

The town has retained some excellent pubs, some with considerable history. The **Malt Shovel** is at 3 Darenth Road, just off the town centre. It dates from 1673 and part of the building was a carpenter's shop in 1643. It was owned by the Dartford Brewery until the business was taken over and in the twentieth century became part of the estate of the large London brewer Barclay Perkins.

Malt Shovel.

The pub has been extended with a large saloon bar and conservatory alongside the car park. Meals are served in the conservatory, while the saloon has polished wood floors, an

Old brewery mirror
in the Malt Shovel.

impressive Welsh dresser and plenty of comfortable seating with leather chairs, sofas and benches. The original bar is small, compact and cosy with a beamed ceiling and an open fire. As well as photos of the pub from earlier years, there's a mirror from the Dartford Brewery that promises 'fine and ales and stouts' – sadly, a promise it can no longer keep.

Since 1982 the Malt Shovel has been owned by Young's of Wandsworth in south London. Young's no longer brews but runs a large estate of pubs. The Malt Shovel sells London Original and Special bitters that are now brewed for Young's by Marston's in Bedford. Guest beers are also available. The Young's ownership is underlined by a photo in the bar of Brian Gould, a shareholder who came to the pub every day. Such dedication!

The Malt Shovel has a strong community role, with regular pub quizzes and barbeques in good weather in the garden. It's claimed to be haunted, with glasses mysteriously flying off tables. Perhaps the seventeenth-century carpenter objects to his former home being used as a tavern, or is Brian Gould unhappy that he can no longer visit the pub in bodily form. The street where the pub stands, Darenth Road, takes its name from the local river that's a tributary of the Thames.

The **Wat Tyler,** 80 High Street, is an even older pub, dating from the early fifteenth century. It commemorates the leader of the Peasants' Revolt, but the name is of recent vintage as it was known as the Crown & Anchor until 1966. The pub has an impressive half-timbered exterior and inside the small front bar is connected to a long corridor that leads to a more spacious back room. The beer range includes a famous Kentish ale, Shepherd

Wat Tyler.

Neame's Spitfire, but with some surprising offerings from further afield including Timothy Taylor's Landlord and Theakston's Old Peculier from Yorkshire.

This is a cheery locals' pub, with regulars greeted as genuine friends, and discussions in the bar range from football results to battles of the Second World War. The Wat Tyler is a good place to spend an hour or two and is convenient for the train station.

DARTFORD WOBBLER BREWERY

Brewing returned to the area in 2003 when John and Miriam Millis moved their brewery from Gravesend to a former cold store at St Margaret's Farm in South Darenth. The ten-barrel plant supplies around forty outlets in a 50-mile radius and the range of beers includes Golden Wobbler, Dartford Wobbler and Country Wobbler. The name refers to the habit in Edwardian times of men setting off on penny farthing bikes from Dartford into the countryside, where they visited a number of pubs and became extremely wobbly on their bikes as a result.

Gravesend

The town of Gravesend, on the south shore of the Thames, has a long maritime and military history. While the pilgrims braved the road, many others, heading for Canterbury, Dover and Faversham, preferred the comparative safety of the river, free from robbers and other ne'er-do-wells. Boatmen offered what they called 'the long ferry', transporting people from London to the town in order to avoid the dangerous highway.

Gravesend had been granted a royal charter to stage a market in 1268. Over the following centuries it developed as a major coaching route and in 1650 the diarist Samuel Pepys, the Chief Secretary to the Admiralty, recorded stopping in Gravesend while en route to the Royal Docks in Chatham. By 1840, seventeen coaches a day were picking up and putting down passengers heading to London or the Channel ports.

As well carrying passengers and goods to and from London, Gravesend ran a ferry service across the river to another important maritime town, Tilbury in Essex, with its major docks. Gravesend needed facilities to load and unload boats and two piers were built in the nineteenth century and survive today as the Town Pier and the Royal Terrace Pier, built in 1834 and 1844 respectively. The Town Pier is the oldest cast-iron pier in the country.

Close to the town are the eerie marshes immortalised by Charles Dickens in *Great Expectations* with such memorable characters as Miss Havisham, Magwitch and Pip, the storyteller who records his rites of passage in the novel.

The pilgrims would not have gone short of food and drink in a town bustling with thirsty sailors and ferrymen. Inns and ale houses supplied their needs and Gravesend in the eighteenth and nineteenth centuries had developed into an important brewing town, with two substantial producers. Walkers Brewery dated from 1780 and it was bought in 1905 by the large east London brewer Charrington. Brewing ceased in 1928 as a result of a major fire. Russell's bought a brewery in 1858 that had been founded by another family in the town. It had twenty-two pubs but this number had grown to an impressive 223 by 1930 when another east London brewer, Truman – second only in size to mighty Bass in Burton-on-Trent – was keen to supply its beer to such a large number of pubs and bought the company. Both the London brewers could transport beer by road or by ferry from Tilbury.

The brewing flag is flown today by **Iron Pier**, Units 6 and 7, May Industrial Estate, May Avenue, Northfleet. The fifteen-barrel plant was created in 2017 by Charlie Venner and James Hayward and they supply thirty pubs in the area. They have an attractive taproom at the front of the brewery where customers can sample the brews on offer and bring their own food, though Charlie and James may add their own pizza oven in due course.

Charlie Venner and James Hayward at the Iron Pier brewery and tap.

As befits a brewery in Kent, their beers are noticeably hoppy and such Kentish varieties as East Kent Goldings and Fuggles are used. The flagship beer is Perry Street Pale (3.7 per cent), while Bitter (4 per cent) uses only English hops. Joined at the Hop Pale Ale (3.8 per cent) uses different hops on a rotating basis and one is always English. Rosherville Red (4.8 per cent) is a popular beer, amber coloured and brewed with rye alongside malted barley. Other beers include a 4.7 per cent Cast Iron Stout and a 5.3 per cent Porter. Charlie and James also have a barrel-ageing programme that includes an Imperial Stout matured in Rioja and Bourbon barrels. A Belgian-style Saison is aged in cider barrels, while a barley wine based on Truman's No 1 is aged in rum, port and Islay whisky casks.

It's an impressive range of beers from a small brewery that's a good twenty minutes' walk from the town centre, though buses go to May Avenue and there's a taxi service a few yards from the train station.

Iron Pier beers can be found, among many others, in Gravesend's most remarkable pub. The **Three Daws** at 7 Town Pier, is next to the historic pier and dates from the 1400s. The ground floor is a function room and you have to climb outside stairs to enter the pub proper. It's a maze of interconnecting small rooms with beams, standing timbers, brick fireplaces, book cases, and paintings and old photos of the area and the pub over the years. One room has a Truman's mirror, indicating the pub was once owned by local brewer Russell's. There are fine views of the Thames with ships, boats and tugboats going about their business.

The pub was first called the Three Cornish Cloughs but the name was changed to the Three Daws – short for jackdaws – in 1745. Over the centuries it has been a haunt of smugglers and press gangs that rounded up customers to join the navy against their will. It's said to be haunted. Today it's a comfortable pub with an excellent welcome from the staff, a good range of meals and a fine range of cask ales, including Iron Pier, Nelson, Shepherd Neame, Dartford Wobbler, Westerham, St Austell and, befitting the pub's history, beers from the new Truman's brewery in London. It's a good place to while away an hour or two.

• Gravesend is famous for its statue of Pocahontas, an American Native Indian, also known by her English name of Rebecca. In 1617 she, her husband, John Rolfe, and young son set sail from London to settle in the Commonwealth of Virginia. But their ship had made just the short trip to Gravesend when Pocahontas was taken ill and died. She was buried in St George's churchyard. A statue of her was erected in 1928 in Jamestown, Virginia, and thirty years later the governor of Virginia presented a replica of the statue to Gravesend. It stands in the churchyard.

Rochester and Chatham

When the Pilgrims arrived in Rochester they would have been well aware of the city's recent turbulent past. It had been at the centre of the Barons' War of 1215, when powerful landowners took up arms against King John. The barons, led by Robert Fitzwalter, were backed by Louis VIII of France. The barons had forced King John to agree to their demands for reforms of his harsh authoritarian rule. A document that carried the royal seal was first called the Articles of the Barons and became Magna Carta, which recognised the rights of landowners, the church and 'freemen', including habeas corpus and fair trials.

The king attempted to renege on his concessions to the barons. When negotiations broke down, the barons went to war. Rochester, built around the River Medway, with links to the sea and to London via the Thames, was of major strategic importance. The rebels captured Rochester Castle from Stephen Langton, the Archbishop of Canterbury, and the king responded by besieging it. Months of brutal battle, hardship and starvation followed; peace was restored only when King John died in 1216.

Rochester today is still dominated by the castle and the neighbouring cathedral, one of the oldest cathedrals in the country. Many ancient buildings have survived from the fourteenth century and there would have been no shortage of inns to accommodate the pilgrims. The guildhall and corn exchange are buildings of great architectural and historic importance.

Much is made of Rochester's association with Charles Dickens. The author lived close by at Gads Hill Place in Higham and the area featured in several of his novels, including *The Pickwick Papers* and *Great Expectations*. Rochester also has the rare, possibly unique, claim of losing its city status. It became a city in 1211 but was stripped of the title in 1998 when, along with Chatham and other towns in the area, it became part of the Unitary Authority of Medway. Efforts are being made to restore its city status.

The Coopers Arms, 10 St Margaret's Street, close to the cathedral and train station, is one of Rochester's many fine and ancient buildings. It has the proud claim of being the oldest pub in Kent, a county that is not short of historic inns and taverns. It started life in the twelfth century, during the reign of Richard I, as a hospice for monks from St Andrew's Priory: the monks were renowned locally for making wine and brewing ale.

The house became a tavern in 1543 following the dissolution of the monasteries and other religious houses by Henry VIII. It was bought by a farmer, Jonathan Qualey, and it became known as the Coopers Arms as it was close to a cooperage where wooden casks were built. The front bar has beamed ceilings, two fireplaces and a

Coopers Arms.

Coopers Arms
bar with a fine
range of beers.

large serving area with a good choice of beers, including a house ale
brewed by the Tonbridge Brewery along with Courage Best Bitter
and Young's Special. A passage leads to a more modern back bar and
a beer garden. The pub has a good reputation for food, including
Sunday roasts. There's live music on Sunday evenings and regular
pub quizzes.

With so much history in and around the pub, it's not surprising to find it has a resident ghost. A cooper who had offended the
rules of his trade guild suffered the dreadful fate of being walled
up alive and left to die. He is occasionally seen in the bar, usually
after customers have supped too deep of the local ale.

Standing proud in the town centre, amid the Dickens memorabilia, the **Two Brewers,** 113 High Street, also has some history on
its side. It dates from 1683 when Thomas Preston was the landlord
and it was built with the aid of timbers from the cathedral: the
beams are now covered over and deserved to be restored. The inn
sign suggests it's named after two draymen delivering casks rather
than actual brewers.

The pub today is owned by Kent's major brewery, Shepherd
Neame of Faversham, and it serves Master Brew Bitter, Spitfire

and Whitstable Bay Pale Ale. The interior is long and narrow and offers comfortable seating with ancient settles where visitors can view a collection of photos of old Rochester on the walls. There's live music on Sunday afternoons and Blues sessions on the first Thursday of the month.

The **Man of Kent Ale House,** 6–8 John Street, is well away from the town centre but is just 200 yards from the A2/Watling Street at the foot of Star Hill, and the

Two Brewers.

Pilgrims may well have passed this way. It bears the name of the major but long-defunct Maidstone brewery of Style & Winch on the glazed tile exterior. The pub dates from 1750 and was first owned by Henry Shepherd. It was taken over by Woodhams Brewery, based in Victoria Street in Rochester, in 1840, and then by Style & Winch in 1918.

Man of Kent.

The pub closed for a while when Style & Winch was taken over and it was a bakery for a time in the 1930s. Today it has one of the best choices of beer in the town and, as befits its name, serves ales only from Kent breweries. The range varies but could include Bexley, Canterbury Ales, Gadds, Goachers and Wanstum. The pub is dominated by a horseshoe bar with ten handpumps serving beer and cider.

The cosy front bar leads to a more spacious room at the back where the local folk club meets for live sessions. It's a cheery and welcoming pub with wooden floors and settles, engraved windows, a wood-burning stove and a wood-fired oven for baking pizzas.

When the pilgrims made the short journey along Watling Street to Chatham they would have found a small village on the coast. But by the sixteenth century, the village started to turn into a major port and dockyard as the English manned the barricades, nervous as always of invasion by hostile foreign powers. The Royal Dockyard was established by Elizabeth I and the town was ringed by forts to further intensify precautions against invasion. HMS *Victory*, made famous by Admiral Nelson at the Battle of Trafalgar, was built there in the 1750s and '60s. In the twentieth century the dockyard became a base for building and housing submarines but, as the country's navy was reduced in size and influence, the dockyard became surplus to requirements and it closed in 1984. The naval buildings remain as a major tourist attraction, Chatham Historic Dockyard.

As ships of the fleet were generously supplied with beer for the crews, it's fitting that a brewery is at the heart of the complex. The **Nelson Brewery,** Building 64, the Historic Dockyard (01634 832828; www.nelsonbrewery.co.uk) celebrated its twenty-fifth anniversary in 2020 and has established a major presence in the Medway area and further afield to pubs and beer festivals. It's been run since 2006 by Piers MacDonald, a former publican with wide experience of the industry.

Nelson brewery
and tap.

Piers has a wide portfolio of beers, all with names with strong
naval connections. They include Admiral IPA, Midshipman Dark
Mild, Trafalgar Bitter, Powder Monkey, Press Gang, Friggin' in
the Riggin', Pursers Pussy Porter and Nelson's Blood. Friggin' is
the best-selling beer, and the brewery is unusual in producing mild
ale all the year round. Tours of the brewery are available between
February and November. Nelson owns a pub in Maidstone, the
Fisherman's Arms.

Railway Street in the town centre is a short road dominated by
two large pubs: as the name implies, the road is also convenient
for the station. The **Prince of Wales,** 1–3 Railway Street, has
an impressive exterior that leads to a large interior with bars on
two floors along with a function room. It's an ideal location for
sports fans, with many television screens. The pub is part of the
Stonegate pub company and it offers good pub food and a range
of beers that include such regulars as Greene King IPA and Sharp's
Doom Bar along with a range of guest beers that often includes
Fuller's and Wantsum.

Over the road drinkers are in the familiar territory of a JD
Wetherspoon's pub. The **Thomas Waghorn,** 14 Railway Street,
is based in a former post office and is named after a naval officer

Prince of Wales.

and postal pioneer who in the nineteenth century claimed to have developed a new route to India from Britain via Europe. The building was acquired by Wetherspoon in 2016 and the group spent £2.2 million refurbishing it. The interior is enormous, with an open-plan bar and upstairs seating. There's further seating in a courtyard garden. Food is the usual cheap and cheerful Wetherspoon's fare and the twelve handpumps dispense such regulars as Greene King IPA and Abbot Ale, Sharp's Doom Bar, a house beer from Rockin' Robin and four changing guest beers, usually with one from Wantsum.

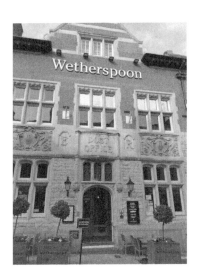

Thomas Waghorn.

Gillingham and Rainham

The pilgrims would have known of the importance of Gillingham when they arrived in the town, for it was mentioned in the *Domesday Book* and had become one of the medieval Cinque Ports created to defend the country from foreign invasion. The town on Watling Street takes its name from a ferocious warlord called Gyllingas who led his troops into battle with great shouting and swearing. The town's name is pronounced with a soft 'g' to distinguish it from Gillinghams in Dorset and Norfolk that have a hard 'g'.

From Tudor times, Gillingham was linked to Chatham, as a substantial part of the Royal Dockyard was based in the town. Its economy was badly affected when the dockyard closed in the 1940s but it has revived its fortunes with a popular marina and a

Frog & Toad.

street market. It's home to Gillingham Football Club, which was relegated to the fourth tier of English football in 2022 and has wide support throughout Kent.

At one stage Gillingham and Rainham formed a single borough but that has been subsumed into the Medway Unitary Authority.

The **Frog & Toad**, 38 Burnt Oak Terrace, is a popular ale and cider house that has won the Pub of the Year award three times from the Medway branch of the Campaign for Real Ale. Visitors are greeted by a large frog and toad motif above the entrance and the single bar is decked out with vintage photos of the area. There are regular beer festivals with a separate bar set up in the large patio garden. Football fans from home and away teams are made welcome. Cask beers include Fuller's and Wadworth but the range is constantly changing.

Will Adams sounds like a modern name but the man who gives his name to the pub was born in Gillingham in 1564. He was a navigator and was the first Englishman to reach Japan in 1600. He settled there and became a Western Samurai. The **Will Adams**, 73 Saxton Street, has achieved the rare distinction of being listed in the CAMRA Good Beer Guide for twenty-six consecutive years and has been run by the same owners for twenty-seven years. There's a samurai theme inside the pub, which has some ceiling

Will Adams.

beams, a darts area and a traditional juke box. The owners open the pub early when Gillingham FC is playing at home and put on special food for fans, including a highly rated chilli. The beer range changes regularly but Oakham Ales are usually available, along with Adnams, Dark Star and St Austell: forthcoming beers are chalked on a blackboard.

Mackland Arms.

The pilgrims may not have noticed Rainham as they passed that way as it was no more than a small hamlet until modern times. In 1801 the population was 422, today it's 6,000 and the growth has been driven by the arrival of the railway that has allowed fast passage to London and Canterbury and towns in between. To assure visitors they are in the correct town, road and station signs announce either Rainham (Medway) or Rainham (Kent) to distinguish it from the town of the same name that was once in Essex but is now on the eastern edge of Greater London.

Rainham has a not-to-be-missed pub, the **Mackland Arms** at 213 Station Road. 'Your friendly local' it says above the entrance and there's 'Welcome' etched on the door. It lives up to the promise. The regulars in the bar give visitors a warm greeting and advise which of Shepherd Neame's beers to sample: as well as Master Brew, there is always a seasonal beer on offer. The pub is dominated by a large horseshoe bar but there's plenty of comfortable seating and walls decorated with fascinating photos, plus many pennants announcing the landlord's support for Ipswich Town Football Club: it's best not to mention Gillingham FC here.

The pub takes its name from the former Mackland Manor House that was home to the Mackay family who owned a printing company in Chatham.

The **Railway** at the station is a more than usually interesting Wetherspoon pub for it's a fine example of the palatial hotels built at the height of the railway boom. It was first a Style & Winch pub before passing to Courage and then to Wetherspoon. The opulent interior, with art deco touches, is divided into many areas by huge timber pillars, all served by an enormous bar that runs the length of the room. The walls are decorated by a plethora of photos and prints that stress the importance of both the railway and the hop industry to the area: there are fascinating photos of hop pickers before mechanisation ended their work, as well as an image of a traditional oast house. The food is the standard Wetherspoon fayre and regular beers include Greene King IPA and Abbot and Doom Bar, with three changing beers.

On the other side of the station visitors can witness an oast house at close quarters, with the familiar white cowls on the roof that revolved in the wind to send breezes into the interior to help dry freshly picked hops. The building is now a community centre.

Hop picking at Frensham, Surrey, nineteenth century.

Preparing the wirework for hops to climb, early twentieth century.

Railway.

Oast house.

Sittingbourne

Sittingbourne was a small hamlet taken over by the Romans, with Watling Street passing through. It was not, however, a place of great importance until the murder of Thomas Becket, when pilgrims rested there en route to Canterbury. By the thirteenth century there were thirteen inns and taverns on the High Street that offered refreshment and accommodation to pilgrims and one, the Lyon, now the Red Lion, remains. Henry V stayed there on his triumphant return from Agincourt. Henry VIII went to Sittingbourne twice and may also have rested at the Red Lion.

Chaucer's pilgrims stayed in the town and it features in the prologue to *The Wife of Bath's Tale*, where the Friar and the Summoner engage in banter:

> The Friar smiled and said, 'Is that your motion?
> I promise on my word before I go
> To find occasion for a tale or so
> About a summoner that will make us laugh.'
> The Summoner answered, 'mine be damned as well
> If I can't think of several tales to tell
> About the friars that will make you mourn
> Before we get as far as Sittingbourne.

In modern times Sittingbourne has developed important paper and brick industries.

Fountain of Ale.

Visitors arriving by train can cross the road for their first pub visit, the **Fountain of Ale**, 37 Station Street. Formerly known just as the Fountain, the Swale branch of the Campaign for Real Ale was formed there more than forty years ago. Not surprisingly, the pub has a railway theme, with signs along the bar for stations in the area, plus Southern Railway and Pullman. The large interior is divided into many areas, including a snug. The pub has an extensive food menu centred on burgers and pizza. Cask beers include Wantsum and Shepherd Neame.

The High Street is a few minutes' walk away and the first stop has to be the **Red Lion** at Number 58. The ancient building creaks with history, with heavily beamed ceilings, standing timbers and bare brick walls. A fireplace with a log burner was once an inglenook, through which can be glimpsed the modern intrusion of a pool table. I doubt Henry V 'got behind the 8 ball' when he visited. Outside, a terraced drinking area is in the yard where coach and horses once deposited travellers anxious for victuals and no doubt a hot bath and warm bed. The current cask beers are Young's Original and Special.

Over the road at Number 41, another old coaching inn has an identity crisis as its owners can't decide whether it's the George &

Red Lion.

Dragon or just the George. The inn sign shows the monarch in full regalia and many coaching inns were named or renamed in his honour. In common with the Red Lion, the **George & Dragon** is rich in history, with bare brick walls and timbers. Adnams Broadside is a regular cask beer.

Other recommended Sittingbourne pubs are: Donna's Ale House, 20 West Street; Paper Mill, 2 Charlotte Street; and Yellow Stocks, 22A High Street.

A few miles north-west of Sittingbourne, the **Three Tuns,** Lower Lane, Lower Halstow, on the A2, is a must visit. This ancient building is Grade II listed and dates from 1468. It was first licensed as an ale house in 1764 and has beams and bare brick walls, with roaring fires in winter. Accommodation is available and landlord and head chef Chris Haines has a fine reputation for the quality of the

The George.

Three Tuns at
Lower Halstow.

food, which includes full restaurant meals, bar snacks and cream teas. There's a large beer garden and a beer festival is held over the August Bank Holiday weekend. The pub has been listed in the Good Beer Guide for twelve years and was named Pub of the Year by the Swale branch of CAMRA in 2021. Regular beers come from Goachers in Maidstone and Three Tuns Best, a house beer supplied by Wantsum Brewery. All beers come from Kentish breweries and include mild, porter, stout, IPA and old ale. It's a dog-friendly pub but they are not allowed in the restaurant area.

Faversham

The pilgrims' joy would have been unconstrained when they arrived in Faversham. They were now just 10 miles from Canterbury and before heading to their final destination they could enjoy the pleasures of an ancient market town with many fine ale houses and taverns with ale supplied by a bountiful number of local breweries.

Faversham was a pre-Roman settlement and, with Faversham Creek, it became an important harbour and sea port. The Romans developed the town, placing it on the Watling Street route from London to Canterbury and the coast. The town became the summer capital of the Saxon kings of Kent and it was sufficiently highly regarded for King Stephen to found an abbey there in 1148. The abbey was dissolved by Henry VIII but a 900-year-old street market by the Guildhall still thrives.

Over the centuries, Faversham developed two important industries: brewing and gunpowder. The manufacture of explosives was vital for the armed forces and the industry survived until the 1930s, when it was closed for fear that an impending world war could see the Germans invading and seizing the munitions. Brewing continues today in the shape of **Shepherd Neame**, officially Britain's oldest brewery, dating from 1698.

There would have been greater choice for the pilgrims. The earliest surviving list of brewers in Faversham dates from 1327 and it records eighty-seven brewsters – women brewers – operating in the town. As the brewsters paid tax it's clear their work was a commercial activity, albeit on a modest scale. Beer making made an important contribution to the town's economy and in 1327, 60 per cent of the town's income came from taxes on brewing.

Shepherd Neame brewery frontage.

Shepherd Neame today is a very modern enterprise, using the latest technology to produce both ales and lagers. But its offices on Court Street, a few yards from the market place, stress the company's age, with oak-panelled rooms, timber framing and old brewing vessels and steam engines from the nineteenth and early twentieth centuries. It could be even older than the official date of 1698: some historians believe the brewery's origins could be as early as 1573.

Shepherd Neame produces an impressive 200,000 barrels of beer a year, runs 323 pubs and hotels and has some 2,000 free trade outlets. The main cask ales are Master Brew Bitter, Whitstable Bay Pale Ale, Spitfire, Spitfire Gold and Bishop's Finger, using the finest Kentish hops. Bishop's Finger refers to an ancient Kentish road sign that points pilgrims in the direction of Canterbury and Becket's tomb. Chaucer's pilgrims would undoubtedly have seen such signs on their journey. The brewery owns a pub in Canterbury called the Bishop's Finger.

Two of the brewery's most interesting beers reflect the intense competitiveness of the industry in the nineteenth century. In 2012 Shepherd Neame's archivist, John Owen, discovered some old leather-bound ledgers in the cellar that contained recipes written in code. It seems the Neames (the Shepherds had long since left the business) were worried that a disgruntled member of staff might cross the road and hand over the recipes to a rival brewer called Rigden. Owen and brewer Stewart Main took several months unravelling the code for two beers, Double Stout and India Pale Ale. The recipes were divided into columns with such groups as GBX, JBX and SBX written in faded copper-plate writing. Main's experience told him the letters referred to the malts and hops used in each brew, along with the amounts. The duo tried all permutations of the letters until they were satisfied they had managed to break the code. Main then brewed the two beers in a pilot plant used to try out new beers.

Double Stout (5.2 per cent) is brewed with roasted malts and pale malt, with East Kent Goldings hops. India Pale Ale (6.1 per cent) is brewed with pale and crystal malts and is hopped with Fuggles and East Kent Goldings. The bottled beers have labels and crown corks that are replicas of the ones used in the nineteenth century. Draught versions are produced as seasonal brews and bottles can be bought in the brewery visitor centre. Rigden's brewery site is now a supermarket. In a series of takeovers, it was bought by Fremlin's of Maidstone and then the national brewer Whitbread, which closed the site.

Shepherd Neame India Pale Ale.   Shepherd Neame Double Stout.   Shepherd Neame Bishop's Finger.

Several of the inns and taverns in Faversham reflect its history. The **Bear Inn,** 3 Market Place, dates from the sixteenth century and was bought by Shepherd Neame in 1736. It's made up of a series of small rooms linked by a passage and has beams, wood partitions and settles. Mind your head as you enter the back room, where the beams are very low. The bars offer Master Brew and Whitstable Pale Ale. Visitors are kindly advised not to use the small

Bear Inn.

room at the front as this is a popular haunt of market workers: it's what German bars call the *stammtisch*, an area reserved for locals.

The **Sun**, 10 West Street, is packed with history. It opened in 1396 and was part of the estate of a local noble. Over the years, ownership passed to merchants and innkeepers until it was sold in 1845 to Henry Shepherd for £800. It has wood-panelled walls, beamed ceilings and large inglenooks, with a frieze of hops above the bar.

In 1793 the Porter Club of Faversham was founded in the Sun and members met there for eighty years. Porter was a popular beer of the eighteenth and nineteenth centuries. It was a dark beer that at first was a blend of three beers: pale, brown and stale, and was first known as Three Thirds. Stale meant beer that was aged for a year or more in large wooden vessels, where it picked up a lactic note from wild yeasts and bacteria

Sun Inn.

in the wood. To avoid blending the beers, London brewers developed a beer with all the flavours of Three Thirds but served from one large cask known as a butt. The brewers called it Entire Butt but it picked up the nickname of porter as a result of its popularity with the large number of porters who worked the docks, streets and markets of the capital. The strongest version of porter was called stout porter, later reduced to just stout. Shepherd Neame's version of porter was popular as imported Spanish liquorice was used for additional flavour. The liquorice arrived in the town from the local port.

During the First World War, the government banned the production of strong dark beers made with roasted grain as it said the energy required to make dark malts should be directed to the munitions industries. As a result, porter and stout became synonymous with Ireland, where Guinness and other brewers continued to make the styles. Today, with no such bans, porter and stout have resumed their popularity in Britain.

The **Shipwright's Arms**, Hollowshore, is a bracing forty-five-minute walk from the town but this ancient inn is worth the effort. It's at least 300 years old and was first licensed in 1738. It served sailors and fishermen working the Thames Estuary and was also a haunt of pirates and smugglers. Hollowshore comes from the name Holy Shore in Viking times. The pub claims to be haunted by the ghost of a nineteenth-century seaman whose boat sank in the River Swale.

The pub has heavy beams and a number of

Shipwrights Arms.

quiet nooks and crannies for customers. Beer comes straight from the cask and includes beers from Goachers Brewery in Maidstone. The brewery was launched in 1983 by Phil and Debbie Goacher, who restored brewing to a town where such major brewers as Style & Winch and Fremlins had been bought and closed. The Goachers believe in using Kentish hops in their beers and they also brew the now rare style of mild ale, which uses local Fuggles hops.

Other pubs to visit include the Three Tuns, 16 Tanner Street. It's Grade II listed, dates from 1605 and was the first tavern bought by Shepherd Neame. Close by, the Bull, 1 Tanners Street, opened in 1409. The Anchor, 52 Abbey Street, is 300 years old.

Places of interest in the area:

The National Hop Collection at Queen's Court has some seventy different hop varieties on show. The land was donated by Shepherd Neame and is administered by Dr Peter Darby of Wye Hops. Kent for centuries has been a major hop-growing region due to the loamy soil that retains a good supply of rain water. The collection includes such well-known English varieties as Challenger, Fuggles and Goldings, along with new varieties Boadicea, Endeavour, First Gold, Jester and Sovereign.

Brogdale Farm National Fruit Collection includes 2,000 varieties of apple, including the varieties used in cider making.

Dr Peter Darby, custodian of the National Hop Collection.

Canterbury

It was journey's end for the pilgrims. After a long and arduous odyssey, during which the miller had contrived to fall off his horse, the party could rest their weary limbs and then achieve their aim of visiting the shrine of Becket in the cathedral. They would have been well aware of the rich history of the city that had started life as a British settlement before being replaced by the Romans, who named it Durovernum Cantiacorum. It was a place of strategic importance for the Romans, based on Watling Street and close to Dover and other important ports.

The Anglo-Saxons followed the Romans and established a community with a large number of refugees from Jutland. In 597 Pope Gregory the Great sent Augustine to Canterbury to convert the pagan King of Kent. The monk was successful and as a result an abbey and a cathedral were built and Augustine became the first archbishop.

Chaucer's pilgrims would have been in good company, for Canterbury drew other believers from far and wide to worship in the cathedral. It remains a place of pilgrimage today, with more than 7 million visitors a year. In spite of the city's deep religious roots, it has known much turbulence over the years. William the Conqueror seized the settlement and built a castle to defend his conquest. In 1381, during the Peasants' Revolt, the archbishop's palace was sacked. But the greatest attack on the city came during Henry VIII's reign, when a priory, nunnery and three friaries were closed. The abbey was surrendered to the crown and was dismantled. Scant respect was shown to Becket. His shrine in the cathedral was demolished and his name and imagery were banned. In 1986 a new Martyrdom Altar was installed on the spot where Becket was slain.

The economy of Canterbury was boosted by the arrival in the sixteenth century of French Huguenots, who introduced weaving and encouraged the planting of hops as they were less than impressed by the unhopped ales on offer. Hop growing, marketing and brewing have been important to the city ever since.

Canterbury was bombed heavily during the Second World War and had to be rebuilt following it. Fortunately the historic architecture was respected and helped gain the city the status of a UNESCO World Heritage Site.

Chaucer's pilgrims would have been impressed by the large number of inns and ale houses that offered them accommodation, food and drink. It's a tradition that has continued to this day, with many pubs of historic importance, including one that brews on the premises in the medieval fashion.

A good starting point for a pub crawl of the city is the **Millers Arms**, 2 Mill Lane, which is close to Canterbury West railway station. The station is on High Speed One, the fast service from St Pancras in London: the journey takes one hour. The spacious pub, run by Shepherd Neame, dates from 1826 and was built to refresh local mill workers. Power for their work came from the River Stour across the road. The pub is decorated with many photos of old Canterbury, the pub and brewing. The large front bar has flagstones and a small inglenook, while the smaller back room is set aside for

Millers Arms.

dining and leads to a courtyard garden. The standard of food is high, as are the twelve bedrooms, each one named after one of Chaucer's pilgrims. The beers are from the Shepherd Neame range and include Master Brew Bitter and Whitstable Bay Pale Ale, with seasonal offerings.

A visit to the **Thomas Becket**, 21 Best Lane, is obligatory. It's just two minutes from the cathedral and greets visitors with an inn sign depicting the martyr in full bishop's regalia. Inside the eighteenth-century building there's one spacious bar with beamed ceilings and standing timbers.

Thomas Becket.

There are images of the pilgrims and old maps on the walls, and there's an impressive oak gantry behind the bar. A tiny patio is set aside for smokers. A mirror from Simonds of Reading on the pub wall is a mystery as the brewery had no known connections with the area, but an etched window at the front bearing the name Rigdens suggests the pub may once have been owned by Shepherd Neame's competitor in Faversham. Handpumped beers include Canterbury Ale's The Reeve's Ale, with Kentish brewer Wantsum's Red Raddle and Taylor's Landlord making a long pilgrimage from Yorkshire.

The **Old Buttermarket**, 39 Burgate, stands opposite the entrance to the cathedral and takes its name from a butter market that once operated on the square that's now dominated by a war memorial. The pub is on a site where an inn has operated for more than 500 years and was most recently a coaching inn called the Black Boy that closed in 1908. The present inn is run by Nicholson's Pubs, a small chain of select historic hostelries throughout the country. It's thought the building may stand on old Roman remains as Roman flints have been discovered in the cellar.

The pub is made up of a series of linked rooms, with a narrow passage leading from the front bar. There are wood and flagstone floors, comfortable sofas, a host of photos of the cathedral and the area and, yet again, murals depicting Chaucer's pilgrims. There's a good range of cask beers, including St Austell Proper Job, Fuller's London Pride, Doom Bar and a house beer, Nicholson's Pale Ale. Bottled beers include St Stefanus from Belgium that's produced by the Van Steenberge Brewery in collaboration with monks at the abbey of Saint Stephen in Ertvelde.

The square is unusual in having two pubs side by side. The official address of the **Shakespeare** is Butchery Lane but the building is divided into a pub and a separate wine bar and the easiest entrance is via the wine bar on the Buttermarket. You cross a courtyard into the pub section, passing a Roman cellar that can be opened for visitors. The pub dates from 1792 but could be much older and has had several names before settling on Shakespeare. The pub is run by Shepherd Neame and has the brewery's range of cask ales, including such seasonal beers as the autumnal Late Red. There's a series of small rooms with wood and tiled floors and much Shakespeare imagery. It's claimed the pub is haunted by the ghost of William Corkine, who was killed in the courtyard by the playwright Christopher Marlowe during a duel in 1594. It's very forgiving of the modern city to name its acclaimed local theatre the Marlowe.

The pilgrims would have felt at home in the **Foundry**, 77 Stour Street, as this is a brew pub with ales produced on the premises, just as they

Old Buttermarket and Shakespeare.

were in Chaucer's time. The pub is run by Canterbury Brewers and Distillers, who produce cider, rum, vodka and gin as well as beer. The building is a former paint supply shop and before that a nineteenth-century iron works. The spacious main room, with an impressive display of hops hanging from the ceiling, leads to a second room with charts explaining the brewing and distilling processes. The brewing kit can be seen through a door and tours are available.

Foundry brewing plaque.

The beers that come straight from brewery to bar include Foundry Man's Gold, Torpedo, Street Light Porter, IPA, Red Rye and Imperial Porter. A Green Hop Festival is staged in the autumn with beers brewed with the first hops of the harvest.

The **Cricketers**, 14 St Peter's Street, is dedicated to the game and has an pub sign depicting two players dressed in 'whites' and brandishing bats while supping jugs of

Foundry.

ale. The pub celebrates the presence of Kent County Cricket Club at the St Lawrence ground in Canterbury, one of the top professional grounds in the country. The pilgrims would have been bemused by the sport and the cricketing memorabilia that lines the walls, including a tongue-in-cheek explanation of the laws of the game, but they would have been aware that a number of games that involved hitting a ball with a stick were popular in their time and those games evolved into cricket, baseball, rounders and hockey. The street called Pall Mall in London, close to Trafalgar Square, takes its name from a game played there called Pall-Mall or Pell-Mell, which was similar to croquet. The Cricketers has a spacious bar with scrubbed floors and offers the full range of Shepherd Neame's beers. Traditional pub food, such as fish and chips and ploughman's, is served and there are regular live music evenings.

Cricketers Arms.

The **Eight Bells**, 34 London Road, is a welcoming pub with a strong local following and a passion for darts. If the pilgrims would have been puzzled by cricket they would have been less mystified by darts as in their time there were games that involved pointed missiles being thrown at targets, while military bowmen would practise their skills by firing arrows at tree stumps with rings and a bull. As you enter the pub you can see the darts area to the left of the L-shaped bar. Five teams play there and their trophies are on display.

The importance of hops and brewing to Kent is stressed by a large photo of an oast house, where hops are dried following the harvest and then sent to breweries. There's also a plaque that advertised stout and ale made by the London brewer Whitbread, which has a dubious

Eight Bells.

record in Kent, having bought and closed the Fremlin's breweries in the county.

The Eight Bells serves Dark Star Hophead and Young's Original. There's a small walled garden, while an area for smokers is known as the knitting circle. The Sunday roast is so popular that booking is essential.

The pub is close to St Dunstan's Church that, curiously, only has five bells. Dunstan was Archbishop of Canterbury from 960 to 978 and he was canonised and buried in the cathedral. His tomb was destroyed during the Reformation. When Henry II started his penitential pilgrimage to the cathedral in 1174 to atone for the murder of Becket, he stopped at St Dunstan's Church to change into sackcloth. The church is a Grade I-listed building.

The **Parrot**, on cobbled Church Lane, is one of the oldest buildings in the city and started life in 1370 as St Radigund's Hall. Radigund (520–587) was a princess from German Thuringia who became the patron saint of several churches in France and England as well as Jesus College in Cambridge. She was a vegan who refused all meat, fish and dairy produce.

The hall was built on Roman foundations in 1370 at the same time as the cathedral was being constructed. It became an inn called the Parrot as a result of a fascination with birds in the medieval period: Chaucer refers to birds many times in his writing and was intrigued by the parrot's ability to mimic human speech.

In recent times, the Parrot was a restaurant for a while but became a pub once again, owned by Shepherd Neame. The ground floor has a mass of beams and standing timbers, with oak floors and several fireplaces. There's a beer garden at the rear and an upstairs function room has further beams and timbers. As well as serving Shepherd Neame's beers, the Parrot has an excellent reputation for food.

The **Unicorn** at 61 St Dunstan's Street started life as a merchant's house in the late sixteenth century. It was known as the Seven Stars at one time before reverting to its current name. Soldiers were once billeted in the inn before a garrison was established in the city. It has a wealth of beams, wood-panelled walls, a curved oak bar and an inglenook fireplace. A back room offers what is now a rare game, bar billiards, and there's a spacious back garden.

Unicorn.

Prints on the wall include Hogarth's famous engravings of Gin Lane and Beer Street, with acute depravation in the former and happy wassail in the latter. One large framed print is devoted to Flint & Sons and their pale and mild ales, porter and stout. The brewery once stood across the road from the pub and was bought by Fremlin's, which had breweries in Faversham and Maidstone. The Unicorn today has beers from Canterbury Ales, Shepherd Neame and rotating guest beers. It's run by a genial Italian, Lorenzo Carnevale-Maffé, who is happy to talk about the Unicorn's history when time permits.

Bishop's Finger.

Close by, the **Bishop's Finger** at 19 St Dunstan's Street, depicts pilgrims on the pub sign being directed towards Canterbury by a roadside finger board. The pub dates from the sixteenth century and shows its

Bishop's Finger sign.

age with beams, timbers and wood-panelled walls. It's owned by Shepherd Neame and there's cricket memorabilia at the front of the main bar with a large mural at the rear showing small casks of ale being attached to planes in the Second World War: the casks were sent to British soldiers in France, who were less than impressed by the local beer (see the Westerham chapter). The pub has a large garden at the rear and there's seating on the pavement where customers can enjoy a pint and watch the world go by. Beers naturally include Bishop's Finger.

Other recommended Canterbury pubs include the Monument, St Dunstan's Street; the New Inn, Havelock Street; and the Thomas Tallis, 48 Northgate. The Two Sawyers at 58 Ivy Lane dates from the eighteenth century and was once owned by the Faversham brewer Rigden. It's a dog-friendly pub with a good reputation for cask beer that may include Black Sheep, Jaipur and Young's. The Old Coach & Horses in Harbledown is on the A2, close to two historic sites, the leper hospital and the Black Prince's Well.

Beer with the Pilgrims in Mind

Martin Guy was well versed in the history of ale and beer when he launched Canterbury Ales in 2010. He had been a 'hobby' or home brewer for many years, specialising in recreating historic brews, including ales from the Tudor period, and when he launched his eight-barrel commercial brewery in Chartham, just outside Canterbury, he was inspired to name his regular beers after the pilgrims.

Canterbury Ales Brewery: Martin Guy and Vanessa Kent.

He was joined by his partner, Vanessa Kent, who gave up a teaching job to work at the brewery. Her name fits well, though she hails from Hemel Hempstead in Hertfordshire, not Kent.

The beer range includes The Wife (golden ale), The Merchant (stout), The Miller (best bitter), The Pardoner (pale ale), The Friar (IPA), The Knight (strong bitter), The Reeve (amber ale), and a Christmas special called The Host, brewed with the addition of ginger. As far as possible, they use hops from Kent and Herefordshire, including the prized East Kent Golding.

Martin and Vanessa have put down strong roots in the area, with some 350 accounts. During the pub lockdowns caused by the pandemic they concentrated on bottled beers, all bottle-conditioned with live yeast, meaning they will improve with age.

Every autumn they produce a 'green hop' beer, using hops plucked from the harvest and placed in a fresh brew. The 2021 Green Gold beer sold out even before it was brewed as a result of demand from local pubs. Green hop beers are the annual equivalent of Beaujolais Nouveau – but so much better to drink.

Martin and Vanessa produce two special beers a month and they like to experiment with styles. To date they have made a Belgian-style Saison and a German Rauch beer, the latter made with smoked malt. Their work has been recognised by the Society of Independent Brewers (SIBA), which gave them a top award in 2014 for The Merchant in the stout category.

Beers.

Becket and Beer

Brewers like to be cosseted and protected. In the old world of Egypt, Babylon and Mesopotamia, gods and goddesses blessed beer and kept it pure. Brewers in medieval England chose Thomas Becket as their patron saint not only as a result of his high status in the church but also as a result of his humble origins as a priest who brewed ale.

Becket was born in London around 1119 or 1120 of wealthy Norman French parents. Following his studies, he was awarded his first post in the church by the Abbot of St Albans in Hertfordshire. While records are vague, it's believed the abbot made Becket the priest in Bramfield, a small village near Hertford. Local historians claim he brewed ale using water from the rectory pond: the pond is known today as 'Becket's pool'. As Becket and his monks washed in the pond, this doesn't sound a very hygienic way to make beer but the water would have been boiled during the brewing process. It's said the rector at Bramfield was still brewing beer with pond water in the nineteenth century.

In 1154 King Henry appointed Becket as his chancellor and in 1157 the visited France on the king's behalf to demand a French bride for the monarch's son. Becket led a colourful parade to emphasise the glories of England. Among the chariots were, according to a contemporary chronicler, two 'laden solely with iron-bound barrels of ale, decocted from choice, fat grain, as a gift for the French, who wondered at such an invention, a drink most wholesome, clear of all dregs, rivalling wine in colour and surpassing it in flavour.'

The ale would have been made without hops but clearly had good keeping qualities: other plants and herbs may have been used as preservatives.

As a result of Becket's associations with ale, following his martyrdom the Brewers' Company in London (which dates from the late twelfth century) claimed it was founded as 'the Guild of Our Lady and St Thomas Becket'.

Pilgrims and Ale

When the pilgrims gathered in the Tabard inn at the start of their journey they would have drunk either ale or wine with their meals. Wine was expensive and was the preserve of the better off, while ale was consumed in large quantities by the general population. At a time when tea and coffee were unheard of and milk and water were full of dangerous bacteria, ale and wine were the only safe beverages to drink. Ale was made with water but it was boiled during the brewing process, killing any bugs lurking in its depths.

While the terms ale and beer are synonymous today, they referred to different types of malt-based drinks centuries ago. The difference was marked by the hop plant. Ale and beer are both made with malted grain, yeast and water. But the ale consumed by the pilgrims in the Tabard and the other inns where they stayed was brewed without hops.

While hops had been used for several centuries in mainland Europe, they made a late appearance in England in the fifteenth century when Flemish weavers introduced the plant to Kent. They preferred the taste of hopped beer – from the German *bier* – to the unhopped ales they found in England. Ale comes from the Anglo-Saxon *alu* and the term was in widespread use in many northern and eastern European countries, while öl or øl were used in Scandinavia.

Ale was made with malts made from barley, oats and rye, with barley the preferred grain. To balance the biscuit character of the grain, brewers added herbs and plants to give some bitterness and additional flavour. In Europe, bags containing a mixture of herbs and plants were known as *gruit* or *gruut*. The habit of adding gruit continued for some time after the widespread adoption of the hop. Writing in 1588, Theodor von Bergzabern said: 'The English sometimes add to the brewed beer, to make it more pleasant, sugar, cinnamon, cloves and other good spices in a small bag. The Flemings mix it with honey or sugar and precious spices and so make a drink like claret or hippocras. Others mix in honey in honey, sugar and syrup, which not only makes the beer pleasant to drink but also give a fine brown colour.' He added that brewers had learned from 'the Flemings and the Netherlanders' that adding laurel, ivy or bog myrtle to beer strengthened it, preserved it and stopped it going sour. As late as 1750, London brewers were still using bog myrtle as flavouring.

Hops, a member of the same family as nettles and cannabis, have a major advantage over other plants and herbs. The oils, resins and tannins found in the cone of the hop add not only delectable aromas and flavour to beer but also play an important antiseptic role in keeping beer free from infection. As a result, hopped beer would stay in drinkable condition for several weeks, while ale would go sour within a few days. To keep ale drinkable for as long as possible, it was made strong, with alcohol fighting off infection. With hopped beer, less malt was used, which cut the costs of production. As commercial brewing started to develop in London and other major cities in the fourteenth century, cutting costs was an important consideration for small entrepreneurs.

In 1574, Reynold Scott published an influential book called *A Perfitte Platforme for a Hoppe Garden* that advised potential hop growers on how to prepare the soil and erect hop poles and trellises for the plants to clamber up and reach out for sun and rain. He stressed the advantages of hopped beer: 'Whereas you cannot make above 8–9 gallons of indifferent ale from 1 bushel of malt, you may draw 18–20 gallons of very good beer. If your ale may

Scott hops.

endure a fortnight, your beer through the benefit of the hop, shall continue a month, and what grace it yieldeth to the taste, all men may judge that have sense in their mouths.'

The ale drunk by the pilgrims in the Tabard would almost certainly have come from the inn's own small brewery. The Rolls of Parliament record that among those taking part in Jack Cade's rebellion of 1450 (see Greenwich and Blackheath chapter) was 'Joh'es Brewersman' of 'Le Tabbard, London'. Tabard, as well as meaning a herald's coat, was also the name given to the lid of a brewing vessel. There's no way of knowing, but it's thought ale at that time was around 7 or 7 per cent alcohol. It would have been brown or copper-coloured. In order to turn grain into malt, it has to germinate and is then heated in a kiln. In the fourteenth century, the fuel used was wood, which produced brown or even darker malt. It wasn't until coke, a product of the Industrial Revolution, replaced wood that pale malts and pale ales were made possible.

It's possible to taste unhopped ale by visiting the Gruut Brewery in Ghent, Belgium. It was founded by Annick de Splenter, a trained brewer or brewster, to use a medieval term. She uses herbs and spices in a wide range of beers. The brewery is open for tours and tastings: Rembert Dodoensdreef 1, 9000 Ghent; www.gruut.be.

The history of hop growing in England can be seen at the Paddock Wood Hop Farm near Tonbridge in Kent. It has displays of hop growing, tracing the period in the nineteenth and twentieth centuries when London Cockney families would spend weeks picking hops as a family 'holiday'. The farm has a collection of Victorian oast houses where hops are dried after picking. The farm closes during the winter: check with the website, www.thehopfarm.co.uk, before visiting.

Hop picking is now a fully mechanised procedure and picking by hand disappeared post the Second World War. The romantic view of cheery Cockneys enjoying a fine time on their hop 'holiday' is not borne out by contemporary evidence, as can be found in George Orwell's novel *A Clergyman's Daughter*. Picking was hard labour, from dawn to twilight. It was back-breaking work, with hands torn by the harsh bines on which the hops grow and stung by nettles. Payment was by weight – the number of hops collected and weighed by the farmers' supervisors. They were ruthless in reducing payments if insufficient plants were picked or the baskets contained grass and leaves as well as hops. There was considerable relief in the evenings when the pickers visited local pubs.

The farm at Paddock Wood was built by the major London brewer Whitbread, founded by Samuel Whitbread in 1742. Three years later he moved to bigger premises in the Barbican, where he brewed just porter and stout. The brewery became one of the wonders of the new industrial age. Visitors, including King George III and Queen Charlotte, went to the brewery to admire the steam engine installed by James Watt in 1785. By 1760 Whitbread had built a porter tun room, 'the unsupported roof span of which is exceeded in its majestic size only by that of Westminster Hall'.

By 1812, under Sam Whitbread II, the brewery was producing 122,000 barrels of porter a year. Vast amounts of hops were

needed and Whitbread bought land in Kent to grow its own supplies. It even developed its own hop, known as the Whitbread
Golding Variety, still grown and used today. The choice of name is
curious as the WGV is a type of Fuggle not a Golding. Whitbread
is not alone in thinking Fuggle – the name of the farmer who first
grew it – is an odd name. In Slovenia, where farmers imported the
Fuggle to plant there, they also adopted the name Golding.

The main hop-growing areas in Britain are Kent and Hereford
and Worcester. The reason is what wine makers call *terroir,* the soil
and climate in which grapes and hops grow best. In the case of
hops, the plants need loamy and sandy soil that retains moisture
and enables the plants to grow at astonishing speed in the spring
and summer.

The British hop industry has enjoyed a major revival in recent
years. Early in the twenty-first century the industry was on its
knees. The acreage devoted to hop growing had declined as more
and more brewers bought their hops from abroad, meeting a con-
sumer demand for the citrus flavours delivered in particular by
American varieties. The crisis was tackled by a dynamic new chairman of the British Hop Association, Alison Capper, working in
tandem with Dr Peter Darby of Wye Hops in Kent. The number
of British hop varieties has grown in just a few years from sixteen
to thirty-four, with several new varieties offering the tangy and
fruity aromas and flavours wanted by drinkers.

New hops developed in Britain include 'hedgerow' varieties
that grow to half the height of conventional plants. As a result
they are easier to harvest and are less prone to disease and attack
by predators.

Peter Darby has developed a number of new hops, including
Boadicea, Endeavour, Jester and Sovereign. There's humour in the
name Endeavour as it was found on his death to be the forename
of the fictional detective Chief Inspector Morse, who was known
to enjoy a glass or three of beer.

Maidstone

Kent is known as the Garden of England and for centuries much of the produce from its bountiful fields, including hops, has passed through the county town. Maidstone is based close to the River Medway, the county's main highway before the arrival of modern roads and the railway.

Maidstone is the county capital with a past that stretches back to Roman and Norman times. The incomers left their mark with roads, abbeys, churches and places of both education and incarceration. Long after the invaders left or were assimilated, Maidstone witnessed mayhem and violence. During the Peasants' Revolt of 1381, Wat Tyler and his rebels freed the radical preacher John Ball, who had been held in prison in the town. A key battle in the English Civil War was fought in the town and ended with victory for Cromwell's parliamentarians. It was the mayor of Maidstone, Andrew Broughton, who was also a government legal officer, who signed the death warrant for Charles I.

As industry developed, Maidstone's economy was based on paper mills, quarrying and brewing. Two of Kent's main breweries, Style & Winch and Fremlins, were based in the town with large pub estates and influential beers. Both fell victim to large London breweries keen to get their hands on the Maidstone firms' pubs in order to fill them with their own brands.

The Medway Brewery was built in 1799 by William Baldwin and ownership passed to A.F. Style. In 1899 Style merged with Edward Winch & Sons of Chatham to form Style & Winch with

365 pubs. In the twentieth century, Style & Winch, with its bucolic image of a farmer and such beers as Farmer Ale and Farmer Brown, bought a number of breweries in both Kent and London. They included the Lion Brewery in Ashford, the Dartford Brewery and the substantial Royal Brewery in Brentford, West London. The brewery had been owned by Felix Booth, who was a distiller as well as a brewer: Booth's Gin survives to this day. He made a large donation to the 1829 expedition that attempted to chart a Northwest Passage between the Atlantic and Pacific oceans via the Arctic. His contribution was marked on maps with such names as Felix Point, Felix Harbour, Brentford Bay and the Gulf of Boothia. As a result, William IV made Booth a baron and the king personally asked for the brewery's name to be changed to Royal along with a royal warrant.

Acquiring the brewery and its pubs was an important feather in Style & Winch's cap but the Maidstone brewery, with important outlets in London, caught the eye of one of the capital's biggest brewers, Barclay Perkins of Southwark. It bought Style & Winch in 1929 with a pub estate of 600 and the royal warrant from the former Brentford site. Brewing continued in Maidstone until 1965, when the plant was demolished.

A second brewery in Maidstone, dating from 1790, was bought from John Headthorn by Ralph Fremlin in 1861. Fremlin disapproved of pubs and closed the ten outlets owned by Headthorn. He concentrated instead on delivering bottled beers to homes using a cart and horse. Fremlin's became the first brewery in Britain to sell large amounts of bottled beer, which included a temperance ale and lager. If the lager used genuine European methods it would have been one of the earliest versions of the style brewed in Britain.

Ralph Fremlin died in 1910 and in 1920 the company was registered as Fremlin Brothers, a limited company. A change in policy led to Fremlin's buying pubs and it also bought a number of rival breweries in both Kent and Essex. By the middle of the twenti-eth century, Fremlin's had become Kent's biggest brewer, with an estate of 800 pubs and was well-known throughout the South-East for its elephant brand beers, including Tusker, Oatmeal Stout, Dinner Ale and Pale Ale.

In 1949 Fremlin's bought another major Kent brewer, George Beer & Rigden of Faversham, originally Rigden (see Faversham chapter). The size and success of Fremlin's came to the attention of the large London brewer, Whitbread who bought the company in 1967 and closed the Maidstone plant in 1972. The Faversham plant brewed a national brand, Whitbread Trophy Bitter, but was finally closed in 1990. In Maidstone, Fremlin Walk is now a shop-ping mall.

Brewing and brewing pride were restored to Maidstone in 1983 by Phil and Debbie Goacher, and Goachers Brewery is now one of the country's oldest small independent breweries. Phil Goacher had worked for Bass in Burton-on-Trent and knew his way around mash tuns and coppers. With his wife, Debbie, he set up a five-barrel plant in an old paper mill in Maidstone and they produced Maidstone Ale as their first brew. It's now called Best Dark and

Howard, Debbie
and Phil Goacher.

has been joined by Real Mild Ale. The dark beers became popular at a time when many were discarding such brands. They are still a regular member of Goachers portfolio and enjoy the growing appreciation of dark beer.

In 1990 Phil and Debbie moved the brewery to an industrial estate in the suburb of Tovil. It's less cramped than the original site and gave them room for expansion. After nearly forty years of hard but rewarding brewing, Phil and Debbie retired and the brewery is now run by their son, Howard.

When he left college, Howard learned the brewing skills with a year's stint at Gadds Brewery in Ramsgate. He's expanded capacity at Goachers to a seven-barrel plant that can produce 1,200 barrels a year. Following in his parents' footsteps, Howard has mapped out a distinctive route to market.

He doesn't deal with pub companies and trades just in Kent and East Sussex, as far as Margate and Rye. Some 98 per cent of sales are in Kent and most of the trade is within a 25-mile radius of the brewery. Goachers makes only cask beer and doesn't have the capacity to produce bottled beer. Howard says he has strong local customers who take four to six casks of beer a week. A dozen casks and he's up to full production.

He's proud of the fact that he buys hops grown in the county – Fuggles, East Kent Goldings and Whitbread Goldings Variety. He uses 100 per cent Maris Otter malt bought from Warminster and Muntons grain merchants. He would like to find Kentish farmers willing to plant Maris Otter, which would 'tick all the boxes with everything grown in Kent'. He adds that the *terroir* – soil in particular – is fine for growing barley.

Back in the 1980s, Phil and Debbie got their yeast culture from Shepherd Neame in Faversham. Howard says the local water is very hard, ideal for pale ales. He treats the water with calcium for his paler brews but not for darker ones.

Goachers has a small estate of three pubs: the **Rifle Volunteers** in Maidstone, the **Royal Paper Mill** in Tovil and the **Little Gem** in Aylesford. The Tovil pub offers lager and bottled beers as well as draught for local drinkers but the other two serve just cask beer. The Little Gem is Grade II listed and was originally part of a manor house. In recent times it was a tea rooms next to a bakery. The Goachers are spending time and money restoring the tiny building. It has an inglenook, ancient beams and a mezzanine floor that will offer additional seating when it's refurbished.

The bar has two handpumps with other beers served straight from casks still aged at the back. The range includes two winter beers, Imperial Stout (4.5 per cent) and Old 1066 (6.7 per cent).

In 2023 the Goachers will mark forty years of brewing and it promises to be quite a celebration.

Little Gem pub.

Part 2:
The Pilgrims' Way

Winchester to Canterbury

While Chaucer's merry band of storytellers made their way from London to Canterbury, other pilgrims trod a different route to the shrine of Thomas Becket. The Pilgrims' Way followed a natural causeway across the North Downs, with Winchester forming a key meeting place for those wishing to make the journey to Canterbury.

Controversy surrounds the route. Some claim the causeway dates from as early as 600 bc, while a counterclaim is that the route is a fiction devised in the nineteenth century. But there is evidence of the route existing in the ninth and tenth centuries and there was mention of a Pilgrims' Way in the thirteenth century. What is beyond dispute is that the route was marked on the Ordnance Survey in 1871 and this led to a number of writers publishing romantic stories about large numbers of pilgrims making their way along the route. Hilaire Belloc was the best-known writer of the time to bring the route to the attention of the public.

The route exists today and is still followed by pilgrims on a regular basis. From Winchester, the route takes in such major and important towns as Dorking, Farnham, Guildford and Reigate, and they have long records of brewing ale for local inns and public houses.

While Chaucer celebrates the London route, a later writer dominates the Pilgrims' Way. William Cobbett (1767–1835) was a prolific radical writer and politician who vividly described the harsh lives of small farmers and agricultural workers in such works as *Rural Rides* and *Country Economy*. As well as calling for changes in the law to stop the exploitation of impoverished rural people, he also railed against the evils of tea and championed the cause of good ale, with his own detailed recipe for brewing at home.

His work is celebrated in a pub in Farnham and a beer shop in Dorking.

Winchester

Winchester, in common with Canterbury, is a city of profound historic and religious importance, with both places linked by the Pilgrims' Way. During the reign of King Alfred (871–899) Winchester was the capital of Saxon England, surpassing London in status. One of the striking features of the city is the statue of Alfred the Great, sword aloft, as he repels Viking invaders.

Visitors today can take in the magnificent cathedral, the twelfth-century castle, the striking Gothic Guildhall and Winchester College, the oldest public school in England founded in the fourteenth century by Bishop William Wykeham and still in its original buildings. The castle houses King Arthur's Round Table, with the names of the knights inscribed around the perimeter.

Winchester, the county town of Hampshire, started life as the Roman Venta Belgarum but its strategic role developed following the Roman withdrawal. Its reconstruction began in the ninth century when Alfred replaced the Roman grid system in order to provide a better defence against the invading Vikings. In the late tenth century the minster was enlarged and it became a centre to celebrate the cult of St Swithun, a Bishop of Winchester, who was claimed to perform miracles. It's said that if it rains on St Swithun's Day the deluge will continue for forty days.

The city had an important Jewish community, marked by Jewry Street. But Simon de Montfort ransacked the quarter in 1264 and in 1290 all Jews were expelled from England.

In more recent times, the novelist Jane Austen died in Winchester and is buried in the cathedral. The city today is considered to be the most expensive and desirable place to live in England. It has a long brewing tradition, with many breweries located in the Hyde Street area, where hard water was ideal for making ale. The last major brewery was the Winchester Brewing Company, also known as the Hyde Brewery. It was founded by James Simonds in 1812 and ownership passed to Richard Moss in 1863. The brewery ran 108 pubs and had an impressive range of beers, including IPA, pale ale, mild, stock ale, porter and stout. It was bought by the Burton-on-Trent brewer Marston's in 1923. Brewing stopped a year later but Marston's maintained the site until the 1980s. It's now a supermarket.

Eleven miles away, the historic market town of Romsey had a famous brewery, Strongs, and a remarkable reputation for drinking. In the early twentieth century, it had eighty pubs, twice the national average: there was one pub for every 151 residents. There's an old Hampshire saying: 'He's so drunk he must have been to Romsey.'

Strongs enjoyed a fine reputation for its beers, which included Dinner Ale, Stout and Golden Ale. It was founded in 1778 and by the 1960s had a sizeable estate of 940 pubs, due to buying Thomas Wethered's Brewery in Marlow, Bucks, in 1949 and Mew, Langton on the Isle of Wight, in 1965. This large estate was tempting bait for the giant national brewer Whitbread, which bought Strongs in 1969 and stopped brewing in 1981. The closure caused outrage among beer lovers.

Both Strongs and Mew, Langton are commemorated with old advertising hoardings in one of the most remarkable pubs not only in Winchester but the whole country. The **Black Boy** at 1 Wharf Hill dates from 1800 and is packed with memorabilia in a maze of rooms served by a large central bar. The name of the pub and its adjoining accommodation called the Black Hole will offend many people and are surely out of place at a time when many statues recalling Britain's colonial past and role in the slave trade are being questioned and removed.

Black Boy.

But swallow your disquiet and marvel at the beams, timbers, bare brick walls and open fires. There's a collection of clocks, memorabilia including old aeroplanes hang from the ceilings and each room has shelves packed with books. A range of stuffed animals, including donkeys and cats, will not suit sensitive souls and a sign saying 'teeth extracted' will recall painful visits to the dentist. On the plus side, the food is excellent and is accompanied by fine cask ales from the local Alfred's Brewery with Saxon Bronze, plus Hop Back Summer Lightning, Flower Pots

Black Boy interior.

Bitter and Flack Manor Porter. A garden offers additional seating in good weather. Take a deep breath and go.

The **Wykeham Arms** is an ancient inn dating from 1755 and, at 75 Kingsgate, is in one of the oldest parts of the city and where a major entrance once stood. The pub is named after a former bishop but the interior pays greater respect to Lord Nelson, with many images of the admiral and his ships: he visited the pub while en route to Portsmouth. The pub previously belonged to Gale's brewery in Horndean, which was bought and closed by the big London brewer Fuller's in 2005. Two beers bearing the Gale's

names – Seafarers and HSB – are
on sale but they are now brewed
at Chiswick. Other beers include
Fuller's London Pride and Dark Star
Hophead. The pub is open plan but
was clearly once made up of several
rooms. There are plenty of inti-
mate areas, with a dining section to
one side. Quiet piped jazz does not
interfere with the buzz of conversa-
tion. Accommodation is available.

The Wykeham Arms.

The **Old Vine**, 8 Great Minster
Street, is at the heart of the city,
opposite the cathedral green. It
dates from the eighteenth century,
is Grade II listed and has an attractive vine-clad facade. Inside there
are oak beams, settles and tables
and, through a curtain, an area for
dining. The pub is well known for
serving meals made with local produce and a range of pies, including
vegetarian, is a speciality. There's a
terraced courtyard and accommodation is available. Beers include
Alfred's Saxon Bronze and Timothy
Taylor Landlord.

The Old Vine.

The **Fulflood Arms** at 28 Cheriton Street is a fine example of
a true community local that's home to crib, darts and quiz teams.
Live music is encouraged with a piano and guitar available. The
large nineteenth-century pub, handy for the train station, has a
half-tiled exterior with signage for the old Winchester Brewery.
The pub is named after the ancient Foulflood, a local stream that

sounds less than appetising. Inside the bar has a wood-burner stove, a library and daily newspapers. Posters depict old Winchester and, if you crane your neck, you can follow a map of the city on the ceiling. A wide range of beers include ales from the micro-plant at the Queen inn, Kingsgate Road, with regular Greene King IPA and Old Speckled Hen and guests from Alfred's and other breweries in the region. No food is served but takeaways can be arranged.

The **Hyde Tavern** at 57 Hyde Street is in the old brewing quarter of the city. It's Grade II listed and dates from 1833, though the low-beamed ceiling suggests it could be far older. The pub has a striking twin-gabled exterior and the interior is comfortable and welcoming, with live folk nights on Saturdays. More music is played in a cellar bar. An excellent range of beers includes Flower Pots Bitter and Harvey's Sussex Best Bitter, with regular guest ales from Red Cat and other local breweries. No food is served but takeaways can be ordered.

The Fulflood Arms.

Steve Haigh has restored commercial beer-making to Winchester with his **Alfred's Brewery** on the Winnall Farm Industrial Estate. Steve is an experienced brewer who worked at Flowerpots, Hogs Back and the Hampshire Brewery before launching his own plant in 2011. He uses a Brew Tech kit from Italy that's based on the European style of mash mixer, lauter tun, brew kettle and hop whirlpool that

The Hyde Tavern.

he feels produces a cleaner and better-quality beer than the conventional British system.

Steve is keen to help the environment and recycles his water and raw materials, and uses biogas made from agricultural products. His base malt is Maris Otter, considered Britain's finest malting barley, and some lager malt, and he is keen to experiment with organic malt produced by Warminster Maltings in Wiltshire.

Steve Haigh Alfred's Brewery.

His main beer, which accounts for 80 per cent of production, is Saxon Bronze (3.8 per cent), a bitter brewed with Cascade and Columbus American hops. The beer has a fine balance of honeyed malt and fruity/citrus hops. Other beers include Winchester Pale Ale (4.5 per cent), brewed with Cascade and Mosaic American hops and Motueka from New Zealand, and Dom Boc (4.2 per cent) made with German and British Bramling Cross hops. The name is Old English and means judgement (dom) and King Alfred's legal codes (boc). Steve also brews an occasional Belgian-style strong ale, High Abbey (7.6 per cent), brewed with pale and crystal malts and hopped with Bramling Cross and Monroe varieties.

Steve delivers within a 7-mile radius of the brewery but 80 per cent of his trade is to pubs within 2 or 3 miles and he has built a strong local following for his beers.

Alton and Four Marks

The market town of Alton and the village of Four Marks will appeal to both beer lovers and steam train buffs. Alton has a 500-year-old brewing history, while both places are on the preserved Watercress train line that runs from Alresford to Alton, where it feeds into the national rail network.

Brewing in Alresford stretches back 500 years. The last major producer was the Alton Brewery that closed in 2015. In the late twentieth century and into the twenty-first it was owned in turn by two national brewers, Courage and Bass, and finally by the global company Molson Coors. In its final years Alton's main brand was Heineken, which ended the contract when Molson Coors acquired the site. When it was owned by Courage it had achieved cult status as a result of a strong ale called Directors Bitter (see panel).

Brewing pride has been restored to the area by the success of **Triple fff Brewery** in Four Marks. It was launched in 1997 by a keen home brewer, Graham Trott, who started with a five-barrel kit in a former furniture factory on Station Approach. Graham sprang to beer stardom in 2008 when his Alton's Pride Bitter won the prestigious Champion Beer of Britain award from CAMRA.

The name of the brewery has a musical link. Triple fff means fortissimo or extra loud, and a number of Graham's beers are named after such legendary rock numbers as Moondance (Van Morrison), Comfortably Numb (Pink Floyd) and Pressed Rat and Warthog (Cream). The brewery has been a great success. In

2000 production increased to eighteen barrels and is now an impressive fifty-barrels kit that produces 160 casks of beer per batch. Graham has two pubs, the **Railway Arms** in Anstey Road, Alton, and the **Artillery Arms** in Hester Road, Milton. He also has a taproom, **Offf the Rails**, at

Off the Rails taproom at Triple fff Brewery.

the brewery along with an online shop.

The beers include Alton's Pride, Moondance, Goldffffinger Lager and Comfortably Numb. The seasonal range is made up of Citra Sonic IPA, Hallelujah Pale Ale, Pressed Rat and Warthog Dark Mild and Winter Cherry Stout.

Musical and other events are held at the brewery: see www.triplefff.com.

The official name of the Watercress Line is the Mid-Hants Railway and it runs for 10 miles between Alresford and Alton. It's best known as the Watercress Line as it once took large amounts of watercress from Hampshire to London markets. It runs regular steam and diesel services and events include real ale festivals. See www.watercressline.co.uk.

Triple fff beers.

Beer that Escaped from the Boardroom to the Bar

The Alton Brewery was run by Courage from 1903 to 1969. At its peak, production was 250,000 barrels in the 1950s. A special beer called Alton Red was brewed for the directors' dining room but a member of staff thought it deserved wider appreciation and he took a sample to a local pub. News of the strong 4.8 per cent bitter spread like wildfire and the brewery decided to launch it as a national brand with the name Directors Bitter.

When Courage sold the Alton plant to Bass, production of Directors moved to other breweries in the group. In 1995 Courage was bought by Scottish & Newcastle Breweries, now Heineken UK. The Courage brands are now owned by the national brewing group Marston's and Directors Bitter is still available on draught and in packaged form.

Courage
Directors.

Farnham

I view tea drinking as a destroyer of health, an enfeebler of the frame, an engenderer of effeminacy and laziness, a debaucher of youth and maker of misery for old age. Thus he makes that miserable progress towards that death which he finds ten or fifteen years sooner than he would have found it if he made his wife brew beer instead of making tea.

William Cobbett, *Cottage Economy*, 1822

Fittingly, Cobbett was born in a pub in Farnham in 1763. The pub was called the Jolly Farmer but Cobbett found when researching his major works *Cottage Economy* and *Rural Rides* that there was little jolly about life in the countryside for many small farmers and their workers. He came from farming stock himself but he became a supporter of radical causes and, following many failed attempts, was elected to parliament as the member for Oldham.

He lived for periods in both France and the United States and supported Tom Paine, the English revolutionary who devoted himself to the revolutions in both those countries. Back in England, Cobbett argued the case for raising wages in order to improve the lives of farm labourers and smallholders, and he supported the right of labourers to form trade unions. In *Cottage Economy*, he set out skills in self-sufficiency for cottagers, including detailed instructions on how to brew their own beer.

Farnham is an ancient town with Roman, Anglo-Saxon and Norman history. Its castle was built in the fourteenth century to provide accommodation for the Bishop of Winchester on his travels in his diocese. The town was much fought over during the Civil War and control passed to both sides during the conflict. Charles I stayed overnight in Farnham when he was brought from captivity on the Isle of Wight. From Farnham, he was taken to London for his trial and execution.

Industries that developed following the Industrial Revolution included pottery, wool, cloth and brewing. In 1860 Farnham United Breweries was formed as a result of the merger of several smaller breweries. The company was bought and closed by the London brewer Courage in 1927 but malting of grain continued on the site for many years: Farnham Maltings is now a community centre.

The Jolly Farmer pub at 4 Bridge Street was renamed the **William Cobbett** in 1971. The large building has several bars and a large beer garden. It shows its age with beams, exposed brickwork and flagstone floors. Regular cask beers include St Austell Proper Job and Sharp's Doom Bar, with rotating guest ales. Best not to ask for a cup of tea.

William Cobbett.

Another pub with some history is the **Nelson Arms** at 50 Castle Street. It was formed from three farm cottages that belonged to the Bishop of Winchester. The name of the pub reflects its connection to Horatio Nelson, who is thought to have visited Lady Hamilton in Farnham. The

The Nelson Arms.

pub has beams, exposed brickwork and a log fire. The beer range includes ales from local brewers Andwell and Hogs Back, together with Timothy Taylor from Yorkshire.

Craft brews.

Craft Brews, The Old Dairy, Pierrepont Home Farm, The Reeds, is a microbrewery just outside Farnham in Frensham, an Area of Outstanding Natural Beauty with two large lakes, called ponds, in 900 acres of heathland. The brewery, first called Frensham, was set up in 2014 by Emily and Miles Stephens in a seventeenth-century dairy on a farm. They added a taproom in a barn with seating inside and out where most of the beer is sold for on-site and take-home consumption. In 2018 the Stephens sold the business to Joe Wood and his partners. Their background is in information technology and the names of some of the beers reflect this. They include GDA or Green Donna Ale, a 3.9 per cent golden ale using Prima Donna hops; USB, a 4.2 per cent bitter with Pilgrim and Northdown hops; i.PA, 5.3 per cent, an India Pale Ale brewed with Endeavour hops; and CAB or Chocolate & Black Porter, 6.3 per cent, using Maris Otter pale malt with chocolate and crystal darker grains. For details of opening times for the taproom visit www.craftbrews.uk.

A few miles from Farnham, the **Hogs Back Brewery** on Manor Farm in Tongham is a large independent operation that enjoys national and international sales. As well as producing prize-winning beers, it has restored hop growing to the area and revived a once-famous variety, the Farnham White Bine.

Hogs Back takes its name from the famous ridge on the A31 and Pilgrims' Way that's 154m above sea level. The ridge links Farnham and Guildford and has views of Aldershot and Woking, with the London Eye in the distance. In 1813, Jane Austen, who lived in Chawton in Hampshire, wrote to her sister about a coach trip to London: 'Upon the whole it was an excellent journey and very thoroughly enjoyed by me; the weather was delightful for the greatest part of the day ... I never saw the country from the Hogs Head so advantageously.'

Hogs Back Brewery was founded in 1992 and quickly achieved success with TEA, standing for Traditional English Ale. When Rupert Thompson became chairman, with a career in brewing that included Bass, Morland and Brakspear, he was keen to use local and natural ingredients with low carbon footprints in his beers. When he researched the agricultural history of the area he discovered that in the eighteenth and nineteenth centuries it was a major hop producer and was more important than Kent or Herefordshire. The Farnham White Bine variety, named after the stalk or bine on which it grew, had a good reputation for the delicate aroma and flavour it gave to beer. When samples were taken down to Kent, an enterprising farmer called Golding planted the

Hogs Back
Brewery.

variety, gave it his name and created one of the world's most treasured hop varieties. Back in Farnham the White Bine was ravaged by downy mildew and other diseases, and the last hop garden in the area was grubbed up ninety years ago.

In 2014, Rupert Thompson bought 3½ acres of land opposite the brewery and set out to create his own hop garden. He called in experts from Herefordshire to build the trellises and wire work on which hop plants grow and he also contacted Dr Peter Darby of Wye Hops, a world-renowned hop expert. Dr Darby has created the National Hop Collection in Kent, where he grows hop varieties both old and new. His research showed that a hop grown in Herefordshire, the Mathon, was a direct descendant of the White Bine and in May 2014 a group of enthusiasts spent a day in the field planting Mathon root stock to launch the Hogs Back hop garden. As well as White Bine, the garden also grew another English hop, the Fuggle, and the American variety Cascade.

Hogs Back Brewery.

It took a year for the garden to produce its first hop harvest. To celebrate, the brewery launched Farnham White, a traditional bitter using only White Bine hops and the variety is blended with other hops in Surrey Nirvana and Hog IPA. Rupert Thompson built

Putting in the Farnham White Bine hops, with Rupert Thompson in panama hat and the author (centre) in dark glasses.

a hop kiln in old farm buildings, where the hops are dried in order that they can be used as fast as possible following the harvest to extract maximum aroma and flavour.

The success of the hop garden led Rupert to move to a bigger 9-acre site behind the brewery. He has added a taproom where visitors can enjoy the beers on site and they can buy some to take home from a large shop. Regular music events and beer festivals are also staged at the brewery. Rupert plans to add a microbrewery where new beers can be trialled by head brewer Miles Chesterman.

Rupert says the White Bine hop garden gives Hogs Back an important point of difference in a fiercely competitive brewing industry and appeals to younger drinkers who are concerned about localism and drinking beers made with grain and hops grown close to the brewery. For information about beers, brewery visits and events go to www. hogsback.co.uk.

Head brewer Miles Chesterman.

Staff cutting down hops bines in the Hogs Back Brewery garden, as harvesting begins.

WILLIAM COBBETT ON
HOW TO BREW BEER AT HOME

Equipment: mashing tub, wooden tub holding 60 gallons. It needs a filter to hold back spent grain. Underback, shallow bucket that slips under the mash tub. Copper, 40 gallon capacity. Cooler to allow wort to cool. Tun tub for fermentation.

To make 18 gallons of ale: two bushels of malt [a bushel is equivalent to 56lb or 25 kilos]; 40 gallons of water; 1½ pounds hops; half pint of yeast; handful of wheat or rye flour.

Fill the copper with water and bring to the boil. Pour boiling water into mash tub. When water reaches

William Cobbett.

170 degrees F [76 degrees C] stir in two bushels of malt. Stir for 15 minutes. Refill copper and bring to the boil. Cover the mash tub with sacking and leave for two hours.

Place underback beneath mash tub and raise the plug. Draw of wort and leave sediment behind. Put wort in copper with hops, rubbing and separating the hops. Boil the wort for an hour. Put boiled wort in cooler, straining out the hops.

Ladle cooled wort into tun tub at 70 degrees F [21 degrees C] or lukewarm. Put half pint of yeast into a gallon container and add some wort as well as rye or wheat flour. Pour into tub and mix well. Cover tub with a sack and stand in a place where temperature is 55 degrees F [12.5 degrees C]. Head will form within six to eight hours and will keep rising for 48 hours. After 24 hours skim the froth. When frothing stops, beer is made. Put into a cask. Yeast will work in cask for a day or two.

Guildford

Guildford has been a town of strategic importance since Saxon times when a settlement grew around the Harroway track that linked Winchester and London. It's thought the town's name comes from gold flowers that grew alongside a ford over the River Wey. Early in its life, Guildford was the scene of a mass murder when Alfred Aetheling or Alfred the Noble, the son of Ethelred the Unready, was travelling with his supporters from Winchester to claim the throne in London. He had been promised safe passage by Earl Godwin of Wessex but the earl was in league with his father, King Harold, and Godwin's forces massacred Alfred's troops; Alfred was kept prisoner until he died. In 1929 the bodies of more than 200 soldiers were unearthed on a hillside west of the town centre.

The town grew in importance when William the Conqueror, who defeated and killed King Harold at the Battle of Hastings in 1066, ending the Saxon monarchy, built a castle of Norman motte and bailey design on the road that became known as the Pilgrims' Way. In 1653 the completion of the Wey Navigation Canal gave the town access to the Thames at Weybridge and Guildford became a centre of the national canal network. The town also became a staging post on the coach route from London to the naval base in Portsmouth. The coach journey took two days and Guildford became an important resting place for travellers. At the height of the coach trade, twenty-eight coaches a day would pass through the town and travellers would seek warmth, food, drink and comfortable beds in five inns: the Angel, the Crown, the Red Lion, the White Hart and the White Lion. **The Angel** on the High Street has survived. The striking building has a Tudor or Jacobean frame with a Regency facade and a medieval undercroft. Guests over the years have included Lord Nelson, Charles Dickens, Lord Byron and Jane Austen.

The coach trade came to a swift end when the railway arrived in Guildford in 1845. The iron way was joined by the internal combustion engine and in 1901 the Dennis brothers opened a car factory that became known as the Rodboro Buildings: it's now a Wetherspoon pub.

Guildford came to worldwide attention in 1974 when the IRA planted bombs in two pubs in the town. When the bombs were detonated, four off-duty soldiers and a civilian were killed. Four men, who became known as the Guildford Four, were convicted and jailed, though they vehemently protested their innocence. They were released in 1989.

The town was home to a large brewery that started life in 1865 as the Friary Brewery. It grew in size and in 1890 it merged with breweries in Byfleet and Chertsey to form Friary, Holroyd and Healy. By 1928 the company owned 400 pubs and in 1956 it merged with a major London company, Meux Horseshoe Brewery, which originally stood at the junction of Tottenham Court Road and Oxford Street, where the Dominion Theatre now stands, though it later moved to Nine Elms. Meux was formed in 1764 and became one of the leading porter brewers in the capital. It went down in brewing history in 1814 when a vat holding 7,600 barrels of porter burst at the Tottenham Court Road site. The resulting flood destroyed surrounding houses and eight people were drowned.

Meux recovered from this disaster but in 1956 it was sold to Friary, Holroyd and Healy to form Friary Meux. The large range of beers included Best Bitter, Meux London Stout, Audit Ale (a

Friary Meux Brewery, 1902.

barley wine), Brown Ale and XXXX. The company went into liquidation in 1961 and was bought three years later by the national group Allied Breweries, which closed the Guildford plant in 1966.

There are two pubs in the town called the King's Head. The **King's Head** on Quarry Street, is close to the castle and dates from the late sixteenth century. It's timber framed with low-beamed ceilings, stone-flagged floors and bare brick walls, with a suit of full armour by the entrance. Images of old Guildford line the walls. It's open plan but with many nooks and crannies and a large patio garden. The pub was bought by Shepherd Neame in 2016 and serves the Faversham brewery's Spitfire, Whitstable Bay Pale Ale and seasonal ales.

The **King's Head** at the junction of King's Road and Stoke Road was originally two mid-nineteenth century cottages that became a beer house before morphing into a fully-fledged pub. It has a spacious interior with ample seating and service from a central bar. A rear extension has been built over an old well and there's further seating in a heated courtyard. The pub serves the

King's Head, Quarry Street.

King's Head, King's Road.

full range of Fuller's beers, including Dark Star Hophead, London Pride, ESB and seasonal ales.

Rodboro Buildings.

The **Rodboro Buildings**, 1–10 Bridge Street, is a Grade II-listed building that started life as the Dennis car factory and became a boot and shoe works. It's now a large Wetherspoon pub over two floors, packed, as is to be expected with this company, with local history and images of Dennis vehicles and the shoe factory. Food is the usual Wetherspoon fare and the standard Greene King IPA and Abbot Ale are joined by local brews from Surrey Hills and Tillingbourne.

The **Royal Oak**, Trinity Churchyard, is also a listed building that dates from 1870, when it was built as an extension to the rectory next door. It's heavily beamed and spacious, with plenty of comfortable seating and an outside area with tables overlooking Trinity churchyard. The pub has a good reputation for food and stages two beer festivals a year. The pub is owned by Fuller's and serves the London brewery's full range of beers, including Dark Star Hophead, London Pride, Seafarer and ESB, with guest ales from Windsor & Eton.

Royal Oak.

Dorking

Dorking, a market town in the Mole Valley area of Surrey, has Anglo-Saxon origins but it flourished in Tudor times when it developed a sizeable industry based on the extraction of chalk and sand. Sand became an important commodity when commercial glass-blowing developed in the nineteenth and early twentieth centuries. The town had a long tradition of non-conformism and supporters included the writer Daniel Defoe. Dorking became a garrison town during both world wars of the twentieth century. During the second war, a committee was formed to help find accommodation for refugees from Nazi Germany and the composer Ralph Vaughan Williams and the novelist E.M. Forster were notable members of the committee.

Farming and agriculture have been important to the town for centuries and the soil is ideal for growing grapes. Denbies Wine Estate was established in 1984 and is now one of the major producers of wine in the country, with grapes grown on 600 acres of land. The estate is also home to a successful independent brewery, **Surrey Hills**, which was founded in 2005 in Shere by Ross Hunter, who moved to Denbies in 2011. The brewery, with annual production running at 3,000 barrels, hit the headlines in 2019 when its Shere Drop Pale Ale won the prestigious Champion Beer of Britain award at CAMRA's Great British Beer Festival. Shere Drop now accounts for half the brewery's output, 95 per cent of which is sold within 15 miles of the plant.

Other beers include Collusion, brewed in collaboration with

Cobbett's, 23 West Street, a beer shop and micro-pub in the centre of Dorking. It was originally a doll's house shop and was launched as a beer shop in 2010 by Tim and Helen Sullivan; the name reflects the fact that Helen is a direct descendant of William Cobbett. The shop and pub are famous throughout Surrey

Cobbett's beer shop and micro pub, with owners Tom and Helen Sullivan.

for the vast range of bottled and canned beers, usually totalling 200, from Britain and overseas. They are complemented by up to five draught beers, drawn by handpumps or direct from the cask. The small but comfortable pub at the back opens on to a garden, where beer can be enjoyed in good weather.

The **Old House** is close by at 24 West Street, which is part of Dorking's Conservation Area. The pub dates from the fifteenth century and it was a former Courage pub until that brewery closed. The pub has a bright and attractive exterior with hang-

The Old House.

The Cricketers.

ing baskets and inside there are wood-panelled walls and bare wooden floors. The bar serves one room but it was clearly once divided into several smaller bars. The beers include Young's London Original and from local brewers including Lanes and SlyBeast. The food is recommended, dogs are welcome and there's a pleasant patio garden.

In spite of the name, **The Cricketers**, 81 South Street, is dedicated more to rugby and has screens that show Six Nations and other major tournaments of the oval ball game. It's a Fuller's pub that's as dedicated to cask beer as it is to rugby, with beers from the Chiswick brewery and its Dark Star subsidiary in West Sussex, including the popular Hophead. Regular beer festivals are held. There are bare brick walls decorated with fascinating old photos of the area along with vintage Fuller's beer adverts. In good weather customers can enjoy a large walled Georgian beer garden.

The **Queen's Head** on Horsham Road is another Fuller's pub that stands out from the crowd by winning the brewery's prized Griffin Trophy as pub of the year 2022 – no mean achievement as Fuller's own an estate of 380 outlets. Manu Bhatt took over the Queen's Head in 2020 and was immediately hit by the pandemic and lockdown but undeterred he invested £70,000 to create an

The Queen's Head.

outdoor dining area with two giant tepees that allow dining to take place all year round.

The pub is a former coaching inn dating from the 1780s and is named after Queen Anne, whose face graces the pub sign. As Manu says, 'she devoted her life to eating and her husband to drinking, so it seems reasonable that she had an inn named after her'. The pub was owned by Friary Meux before becoming a Fuller's house. Food is of the highest quality, there are fine wines and the beers are from the Fuller's range.

Reigate

Pilgrims are by nature wandering folk but the **Pilgrim Brewery** on West Street in Reigate has put down deep roots in the Surrey town. It's a brewery that has played a key role in the history of modern brewing in both Surrey and beyond. It was founded in 1982 by Dave Roberts, who used his skills as an engineer to build a plant that restored brewing to a county that had lost such major producers as Friary Meux and King & Barnes.

And as a former civil servant, Dave was able to direct members of SIBA, the Small Independent Brewers' Association – now the Society of Independent Brewers – to the most important policy makers in government to discuss reform of excise duty. The result was Progressive Beer Duty, introduced in 2002, that cut beer tax for small producers and enabled the micro section of the industry to flourish.

Pilgrim Brewery.

Pilgrim beers.

Dave celebrated Reigate's history with such beers as Progress, Talisman – named after the shells pilgrims carried for good luck – and a strong ale of 8.7 per cent called Crusader.

Dave retired in 2017 and the business was bought almost by chance by Adrian Rothera and Rory Fry-Stone. Rory lives close to the brewery on West Street and dropped in one day and heard that Dave wanted to sell the business. He says he only went into buy some beer and left having made an offer on the brewery.

Both Rory and Adrian had worked for local family firms. They shared a love of beer and had discussed the possibility of joining forces to run their own business. They threw themselves into a much-needed upgrade of the plant and they added a taproom that has enabled locals to enjoy the beer on site. They were joined by head brewer John Fridd, who had previously worked at the Cottage Brewery in Somerset. He has busily enlarged the beer range and added craft keg, bottles and cans to the cask beers. Cask accounts for 85 per cent of output and John stresses that his keg beers are unfiltered and as close to cask as possible.

In 2018 the brewery closed for a month for refurbishment. A new floor and drainage were installed along with air conditioning in the cold store, where 300 casks are kept. The original mash tun and hot liquor tank have been retained but the plant has a new copper and cask washer, while the number of fermenting vessels has increased from three to five. It's now a twelve-barrel operation, producing 200 casks a week, and the growth has been necessary to keep up with demand.

As well as selling to around two dozen pubs in the area, the taproom has been a runaway success. People in Reigate didn't realise they had a local brewery, Rory says. The taproom put Pilgrim firmly on the map, to such an extent that at one stage the brewery was close to running out of beer. As well as drinking on the premises, customers can take beer home and the take-home side of the business has boomed as a result.

Pilgrim has formed a lucrative deal with Surrey County Cricket Club. The club takes Pilgrim beers and at one five-day Test match at the Oval it sold 300 casks. Not bad for a microbrewery, Rory laughs.

When the Covid pandemic struck, Pilgrim survived the lockdown by brewing twice a week and building take-home sales. It's now working full bore again and supplying free trade pubs.

Rory says they are maintaining the heritage of the brewery with the core range but are also developing new beers. Dave Roberts' Progress remains the bestseller in cask and keg, with the keg version supplied mainly to local clubs. But it's been joined by IPA, an American-style NEIPA – New England India Pale Ale – a golden ale, stout and lager, and many seasonal and occasional brews.

Whatever the style, Rory insists that only the finest malts and hops are used. In the spick-and-span brewhouse, John Fridd says he uses Maris Otter as his base malt along with Flagon and Propena, with Pils malts for his lager. For a smoked beer he imported special grain from Weyermann Malt in Bamberg in Germany. Depending on the style, John has a malt store holding crystal, chocolate, rye, oats and wheat malts, along with roasted barley.

Hops include Whitbread Goldings Variety and Challenger from this country, with Hersbrucker from Germany, Bobek from Slovenia and American Cascade, Chinook, Citra and Mosaic.

The **Bell Inn**, 21 Bell Street, is an ancient pub with a small frontage but it has a long and narrow bar inside with a low ceiling, wooden floor and an old Ordnance Survey map on the ceiling.. There's a heated patio at the rear. Food is made with locally sourced ingredients and the beers include Greene King IPA, Old Speckled Hen and seasonal from the Greene King range.

The Bell.

Westerham

The **Westerham Brewery** was opened by Robert Wicks in 2004 and as well as brewing a wide range of modern beers, Robert has also recreated a number of ales associated with a former major brewery in the town, Black Eagle.

Westerham Brewery founder Robert Wicks with his torpedo special vessels.

The town of Westerham has a brewing tradition stretching to the early 1600s. Black Eagle was founded in 1841 by Robert Day, who used the local waters to fashion pale ales while he brewed porter in Bermondsey, where London's soft water was better-suited to making dark beers.

The Westerham plant was sufficiently successful to have a special branch line of the railway built for it in the late nineteenth century. Trains came from Sevenoaks and carried beer to London and back. In the twentieth century the brewery had to make a much shorter journey to deliver beer to Chartwell, the country home of Sir Winston Churchill, just 2 miles away. Churchill is thought of as primarily a Cognac drinker but he enjoyed beer as well.

The brewery played a key role during the Second World War. Its beers were popular with airmen based at the Biggin Hill base and this led to collaboration between Black Eagle and the Royal Air Force to supply beer to troops fighting the Germans in Normandy. The brewery delivered draught beer to Biggin Hill, where it was pumped into auxiliary 18-gallon fuel tanks fitted beneath the wings of Spitfires. Mild ale was in the tanks on one side of the plane, bitter on the other side. The tanks were labelled 'Modification XXX Depth Charges' in order to be approved by the air force authorities, who may not have known – or turned a blind eye to the fact – that the use of Xs was a common way of branding beers in those days. The flights were called Beer Runs and they were enormously popular with British troops, who had expressed their dissatisfaction with French beer.

Black Eagle was bought in 1948 by a London brewery, Taylor Walker in Limehouse. The 1960s saw a wave of consolidation in the industry and in 1964 Taylor Walker was taken over by Ind Coope, a major brewery with plants in Romford, Essex, and Burton-on-Trent. Ind Coope closed the Black Eagle site a year later, though it used it for warehousing and distribution for a few years.

Robert Wicks has restored brewing in Westerham, along with some of the Black Eagle beers and others inspired by the old brewery's brands. Robert is keen to cut down on carbon miles and he uses local materials as far as possible. His brewing water percolates through the Lower Greensand Ridge and is perfect for brewing pale ales and bitters. He has his own bore hole on site, drilled down 90m.

He is a proud user of Kentish hops and 90 per cent of the hops used in his beers come from within the county. He sources them at the Scotney Castle Estate at Lamberhurst and Finchcocks hop gardens in Goudhurst. There are nine different hops in Westerham's flagship beer, Spirit of Kent (4 per cent).

Robert's grains come from further afield, as Kent is not a major barley-growing region. Maris Otter pale malt – considered to be the finest malting barley – comes from Crisp Malt in Norfolk, with coloured malts from French and Jupp in Hertfordshire. For recreations of Black Eagle beers, Robert sourced original yeast strains deposited at the National Collection of Yeast Cultures in Norwich.

British Bulldog (4.1 per cent) is a new beer, not a recreation, but it celebrates Black Eagle's legacy and the Churchill connection: the pump clip shows the former prime minister's famous two-fingered victory sign. The hops are Northdown and Whitbread Goldings Variety and the beer is pumped through a device called the Hop Rocket. This is a steel tube packed with hops from which the beer picks up additional aroma, flavour and bitterness. The varieties used in the rocket are Goldings and Progress.

The bitter 1965 (4.8 per cent) marks three events in that year: the closure of Black Eagle, the death of Churchill and Robert Wicks's birth. The hops are Goldings and Northdown.

Audit Ale (6.2 per cent) is based on a Black Eagle recipe from 1938. The brewery produced Audit Ale for a number of London colleges that held special feasts to mark the annual audit of their accounts. The beer is brewed with pale and crystal malts and is hopped with Goldings and Northdown. It has a big spicy and fruity character with notes of molasses, raisins and port wine. It's thought Audit Ale was also supplied to Churchill at Chartwell, who wasn't deterred by the strength of the beer. As he once said: 'I have taken more out of alcohol than alcohol has taken out of me.'

Westerham Audit Ale.

Westerham brews a number of seasonal beers alongside its regular ones. As well as pubs throughout Kent and beyond, the brewery has a popular taproom and shop where beer tastings and other events are held, including street food supplied by local caterers. Brewery tours are available. Westerham Brewery, Beggars Lane, Westerham TN16 1QP; www.westerhambrewery.co.uk.

Also in Westerham, visit the **Real Ale Way,** 23 High Street, which serves the brewery's beers along with beers from Larkins and Tonbridge breweries. Forthcoming beers are shown on a board next to the bar. Stairs led to a cosy retreat on the first floor that also serves a function room.

Spitfire being loaded with beer. (Courtesy Eric B. Morgan and Edward Shacklady)

Notes and Acknowledgements

Extracts from Chaucer's *The Canterbury Tales* come from Nevill Coghill's translation in modern English (Penguin Books). It was first published in 1951 and has been in continuous publication ever since.

Thanks are due to branches of CAMRA, the Campaign for Real Ale, in Kent and Surrey, for their recommendations for pubs. Special thanks are due to Gill and Gerry Keay and Joe Mist in Canterbury for help beyond the call of duty; and Stephen and Christine Rayner for a memorable tour of Rochester.

Extra special thanks are due to Kathryn Tye and Rose Davis at Shepherd Neame for their generous time, help and hospitality.

The final choice of pubs is mine and I am responsible for any errors. Please note that the range of beers available in a pub can change, especially when it's a free house not owned by either a brewer or a pub company.

Most contemporary photographs were taken by the author. Some were supplied by brewers or publicans, while others are courtesy of CAMRA's www.whatpub.com. Special thanks to Ros Shiel of Shiel Porter Public Relations for images of hop planting and growing at Hogs Back Brewery in Tongham.